Presenta:

Let's Start Talking
Fundamentos de Inglés

Un guía para principiantes para hablar inglés

Authors:

David Stevens | Frances Holder

Editing and Proofreading by:

Pedro Vallejo | Irina Sposito

Table of Contents

BrightView está empleando en Parker, Colorado!

Actualmente estamos solicitando:

- **Obreros del paisaje**
- **Líderes de Equipo**
- **Encargados de Jardineros Paisajistas**

El pago comienza en $16.07/hora. A medida que crezca con la empresa y sus habilidades de comunicación bilingües mejoren, ¡su salario también aumentará!

¡BrightView está comprometido con tu éxito con el inglés!

Además de trabajar para una gran empresa de paisajismo, trabajar en BrightView le dará muchas oportunidades para practicar inglés. Tendrá oportunidades diarias para traducir del español al inglés y viceversa, ya que empleamos a casi el mismo número de hablantes nativos de español e hablantes nativos de inglés. También alentamos y apoyamos a nuestros empleados para que aprendan ambos idiomas.

¡Nuestra compañía ha estado enviando empleados a The Language School desde 2018 para aprender ambos idiomas, y estamos encantados de ofrecer oportunidades de empleo a los estudiantes de The Language School!

A medida que su competencia con el inglés mejora, ofrecemos varias trayectorias de carrera hacia títulos más altos y salarios más altos.

Aplique en línea - Asegúrese de seleccionar PARKER en la opción para "ciudad"

https://jobs.brightview.com/

Para preguntas relacionadas con el proceso de solicitud, llame o envíe un mensaje de texto a Paulina Ochoa: (720) 629-8544

Acerca de BrightView | El Comienzo de Algo Grande

Únase a la compañía de servicios de paisajismo líder en el sector, con un equipo de 22,000 miembros para los que cuidarse entre sí es tan importante como cuidar a los clientes. A medida que diseñamos, desarrollamos, mantenemos y mejoramos los paisajes de todo el país, creamos nuevas oportunidades y concretamos grandes sueños. El éxito comienza aquí.

¡Romero's Foundation Inc. está contratando trabajadores bilingües español/inglés en Aurora, CO!

Siempre estamos necesitando las siguientes posiciones:

- **Conductores comerciales (CDL) Clase A**
- **Conductores comerciales (CDL) Clase B**
- **Operadores de bombas de concreto**

- **Trabajo de pavimentación**
- **Trabajo de acabado de concreto**
- **Trabajo de cimentación de concreto**
- **Posiciones laborales de temporada**

El pago inicia en $18.00-$32.00/hora.

Acerca de Romero's Foundation:

Romero's Foundation ha estado en el negocio desde 2008, ofreciendo trabajos en concreto para construcciones residenciales nuevas realizadas por reconocidos constructores locales. El dueño, el Sr. Gerardo Romero, ha construido su empresa uniendo su origen hispánico con trabajo duro y sacrificio. El Sr. Romero tuvo que aprender inglés para poder tener éxito en este país. Ser bilingüe le ha abierto muchas puertas a él y a su negocio.

Ahora su meta principal es dar a otros la oportunidad de crecer profesionalmente en su empresa.

Para todos aquellos quienes quieran ser parte de una compañía en crecimiento con una excepcional ética laboral, y además tener la oportunidad de practicar inglés y español, ¡postúlese hoy!

Por favor contacte a Daryl McCormick vía correo electrónico a DarylM@Romerosfoundation.Net o contáctenos en nuestra oficina al:

720.456-6453
Romero's Foundation Inc.
14211 E. 4th Ave, Bldg. 3 Ste #133
Aurora CO 80011

¡Hospital Cooperative Laundry está contratando!

¡Hospital Cooperative Laundry, la lavandería comercial de atención médica más grande de Colorado, ahora está contratando! Actualmente, servimos a más de 400 clínicas médicas, hospitales y centros cirujanos con un volumen anual de 50 millones de libras procesadas. ¡Hospital Cooperative Laundry ofrece increíbles beneficios, empleo a tiempo complete y oportunidades de crecimiento!

MÚLTIPLES POSICIONES DISPONIBLES

- Trabajador de producción
- Primer y segundo turno
- Conductor de camión de entregas
- Técnico de mantenimiento
- Conserje

- Asociado de distribución hospitalaria en un hospital cerca de usted
- Líder de distribución hospitalaria
- Asociado "flotante" de distribución hospitalaria
- Supervisor de distribución hospitalaria

BENEFICIOS

- Primer día del mes luego de 60 días:
  - Atención médica
  - Atención odontológica
  - Atención oftalmológica

- Bonos de recomendación **ILIMITADOS**

- Pago de feriados

  - Protección en caso de accidente
  - Protección por discapacidad

- Plan de ahorros 401K con una generosa igualación de la compañía después de un año de servicio
- Vacaciones después de un año de servicio

Postúlese en línea en www.hospitalcooperative.com o visítenos en 6225 East 38th Avenue, Denver, CO 80207.

Patrocine
Let's Start Talking –
Fundamentos de Inglés

- **¿Necesita reclutar empleados bilingües que hablen tanto inglés como español?**
- **¿Está tratando de expandir sus productos o servicios en un mercado hispanoparlante?**

The Language School está buscando reducir el costo de estudiar inglés para sus alumnos, ¡y está ofreciendo a las empresas locales oportunidades únicas de patrocinio para ayudarnos a contrarrestar estos costos! Si tiene un producto, servicio, o trabajo en el cual quisiera hispanoparlantes que estudien inglés en Denver, y lo quiere dar a conocer, esta es una gran oportunidad para usted.

Para más información contacte:

David Stevens, Director of The Language School
david@TheLanguageSchool.us
(720) 257-8539

For Teachers - How to use this book:

This book has been used at The Language School to teach thousands of students how to speak English and you can do the same! Each lesson includes new vocabulary, grammar, and conversational activities that you can use to lead the class.

For best results, The Language School recommends that this book be used for group classes that have no more than 10 students, or for private instruction. You should also buy the accompanying PowerPoint presentations for $99 in order to easily lead conversational classes with your students. With the books and presentations, ***there will be no need to spend time preparing for class again!***

The lessons included in this book should be conducted by using the presentations, and they should be done 100% orally during your class with your students. Students can then complete the lessons included in this book at home as homework.

For your students' convenience, flashcards are included at the end of each chapter. Have your students cut them out at the end of class and spend some time reviewing the vocabulary together.

For more information on the accompanying PowerPoint presentations, contact The Language School today:

www.TheLanguageSchool.us
info@thelanguageschool.us
(720) 634-2589

Stop spending time preparing new English lessons! With The Language School's PowerPoint presentations, each lesson has been designed to enable you to simply show up and teach.

Presentándonos

1. What is your name?
   - My name is _____.
2. Where are you from?
   - I am from _____.

Each lesson is filled with conversational activities through which you can guide the students through or have them take turns asking and answering the questions they see.

Review: BE

Hi, my name _____ James. I _____ from New York City, but now I live in Denver, CO. I have two brothers. One _____ older than me and his name _____ Kenneth. Kenneth _____ an English Teacher. My younger brother _____ 21 years old and he _____ studying business at the University of Colorado. His name _____ Matt. My brothers _____ very busy and we only see each other during holidays.

My parents _____ from Mexico. We try to speak Spanish when we _____ together. Our family _____ very close, and we talk on the phone every day. My dad _____ funny, and my mom _____ always optimistic.

My wife _____ an artist and she _____ from Brazil. We have two daughters and they _____ beautiful and intelligent. I _____ happy because I have a great family!

Review: BE

Hi, my name _is_ James. I _____ from New York City, but now I live in Denver, CO. I have two brothers. One _____ older than me and his name _____ Kenneth. Kenneth _____ an English Teacher. My younger brother _____ 21 years old and he _____ studying business at the University of Colorado. His name _____ Matt. My brothers _____ very busy and we only see each other during holidays.

My parents _____ from Mexico. We try to speak Spanish when we _____ together. Our family _____ very close, and we talk on the phone every day. My dad _____ funny, and my mom _____ always optimistic.

My wife _____ an artist and she _____ from Brazil. We have two daughters and they _____ beautiful and intelligent. I _____ happy because I have a great family!

Review: BE

Hi, my name _is_ James. I _am_ from New York City, but now I live in Denver, CO. I have two brothers. One _____ older than me and his name _____ Kenneth. Kenneth _____ an English Teacher. My younger brother _____ 21 years old and he _____ studying business at the University of Colorado. His name _____ Matt. My brothers _____ very busy and we only see each other during holidays.

My parents _____ from Mexico. We try to speak Spanish when we _____ together. Our family _____ very close, and we talk on the phone every day. My dad _____ funny, and my mom _____ always optimistic.

My wife _____ an artist and she _____ from Brazil. We have two daughters and they _____ beautiful and intelligent. I _____ happy because I have a great family!

Fill in the blank activities automatically populate with the correct answer. Simply have the students read through the sentences and tell you the right answer. Advance the slide and they can instantly see if they are right!

Acerca del libro:

Let's Start Talking! Fundamentos de Inglés 1 es el primer curso de inglés de una serie de clases conversacionales en inglés creadas por The Language School. Este curso está diseñado para ayudar a adultos a comenzar a hablar en inglés:

- en el trabajo,
- en sus comunidades locales,
- y mientras viajan por el mundo angloparlante (incluidos EEUU, Canadá e Inglaterra).

Una vez complete este curso, usted tendrá una base sólida de inglés. Sus nuevas habilidades conversacionales en inglés incluirán ser capaz de presentarse, ordenar comida en un restaurante e ir a comprar productos básicos. Finalmente, usted sabrá cómo comenzar conversaciones simples en inglés con angloparlantes nativos.

Además de sus nuevas habilidades conversacionales, usted también aprenderá acerca de varias culturas que existen en el mundo angloparlante, para que así no solo hable inglés, sino que también entienda las costumbres de los diferentes países y pueda socializar con sus nuevos amigos.

Características resaltantes de

Let's Start Talking! Fundamentos de Inglés 1

- Greetings   (Saludos)
- Restaurants   (Restaurantes)
- Shopping   (Compras)
- Culture   (Cultura)
- Conversation   (Conversación)

Acerca del autor: David Eugene Stevens III:

La misión de vida de David está dedicada a ayudar a otros a aprovechar todo su potencial a través de la educación, comunicación y crecimiento espiritual, lo cual tendrá un impacto positivo en nuestro mundo y fortalecerá nuestras comunidades.

David comenzó a enseñar inglés en el 2001 y español en el 2005, y luego fundó The Language School en Denver, Colorado, en 2007 para compartir su conocimiento sobre nuevos lenguajes y culturas. Desde ese entonces ha publicado varias series de libros teóricos y prácticos para ayudar a las personas a aprender tanto español como inglés.

Él está comprometido con ayudar a las personas a mejorar sus vidas al aprender nuevos idiomas como inglés, español, francés e italiano. Él cree que una buena educación es la cosa más importante que una persona puede obtener y que debería ser divertida, asequible y accesible para todos. Tiene un título universitario en Comercio Internacional y Español del Eckerd College, donde se graduó de primero en su promoción. Su experiencia internacional incluye haber vivido, estudiado y viajado a países de América Latina, Europa y Asia.

Acerca de The Language School

The Language School enseña inglés y español conversacional a adultos, para que de esta forma los estudiantes puedan hablar el nuevo lenguaje con confianza en sus trabajos y comunidades o durante sus viajes.

Ubicada en Denver, Colorado, ofrecemos una variedad de formas de estudiar, incluyendo grupos de clase pequeños, lecciones privadas y programas de inmersión intensivos.

The Language School ofrece el enfoque *Let's Start Talking*™ para aprender nuevos idiomas. Esto significa clases conversacionales en inglés y en español para que usted pueda comenzar a hablar con confianza en el trabajo, en su comunidad o durante sus viajes.

Enseñamos en configuraciones de grupos pequeños, ¡lo cual les ofrece a nuestros estudiantes la confianza que necesitan para comenzar a hablar! Es un enfoque natural y práctico para aprender un nuevo idioma y está basado en las conversaciones del día a día.

Nuestro estilo de clases conversacionales crea un ambiente cálido y dinámico para el aprendizaje de un idioma. Los estudiantes y profesores se divierten, y nuestros estudiantes aprenden lo que realmente necesitan aprender.

Para más información, por favor contacte a:

www.TheLanguageSchool.us

Phone: +1 (720) 634-2589

Introducción

Gracias por elegir The Language School como recurso de aprendizaje para aprender el idioma inglés. Aprender inglés no quiere decir solamente aprenderlo para comunicarse, sino también para adaptarse eficientemente a una nueva cultura, por lo que le aseguramos que aprenderá mucho más que solo una lengua en nuestro centro de idiomas. ¡Además de eso, nuestra filosofía es que debe ser fácil y divertido!

Nuestros instructores cuentan con un alto nivel de educación superior en pedagogía y tienen también vasta experiencia enseñando idiomas. Así que puede estar seguro de que The Language School le ayudaremos a alcanzar sus metas de hablar, escribir y entender el inglés con fluidez.

Objetivos

Las personas generalmente quieren aprender inglés por razones personales o profesionales. Escribir sus metas le puede ayudar a sentirse motivado mientras aprende inglés.

Por favor, tómese unos minutos para decirnos porqué ha decidido estudiar inglés en The Language School:

Personal

1.)_____

2.)_____

3.)_____

Profesional

1.)_____

2.)_____

3.)_____

Consejos para estudiar Inglés

CONSEJOS DE ESTUDIO
PARA APRENDER A HABLAR
INGLÉS

Presentado por:

The Language School

Let's Start Talking

www.TheLanguageSchool.us
info@TheLanguageSchool.us
(303) 997-9207

¡Libro electrónico gratis! Como agradecimiento especial por usar este libro, queremos darle un regalo gratis para ayudarlo a desarrollar la fluidez lo más rápido posible.

Envíe un correo electrónico a info@TheLanguageSchool.us con el asunto:

Envíeme el libro electrónico gratuito "Consejos de estudio para aprender a hablar español"

Lesson 1/Lección 1

Lesson Highlights:

New (Nuevo):
El objetivo principal del primer nivel es enseñarte cómo presentarte bien en inglés, o en inglés: *introduce yourself.*

- Greetings   (Saludos)
- Culture tip: How to greet people   (Consejo de la cultura: Cómo saludar)
- Conversation tip: Cognates   (Cognados)
- Vowels/Pronunciation   (Vocales)
- The Alphabet   (El alfabeto)
- Numbers (0-10)   (Los números)
- Vocab: Work and School   (El trabajo y la escuela)

Nuevo: Saludos/Greetings

Vamos a ver un video para ver lo que vamos a aprender hoy:

https://youtu.be/kisbgc8-fvU

New: Cultura y saludos

Cuando estás aprendiendo un idioma nuevo, es igualmente importante aprender la cultura que lo acompaña. Por ejemplo, cuando saludas a una persona en otros países, puede ser hecho de una manera distinta que la costumbre de tu país.

En los Estados Unidos *a hug*, o un abrazo, es normal en situaciones informales. Esto puede pasar entre:

- hombre y hombre
- mujer y mujer
- hombre y mujer

En situaciones formales un handshake, o un apretón de manos, es normal. Piensa en ocasiones como

- Reuniones de negocios
- Conocer a una persona por la primera vez

Por su puesto, no esté sorprendido si se encuentra en cualquiera de las situaciones de arriba y el saludo es realizado diferente. Los saludos pueden cambiar dependiendo de la subcultura de la persona. Estados Unidos es multicultural y hay gente de varias demográficas socioeconómicas, pues hay personas más amigables y otras más formales. Antes de llegar a Estados Unidos, es importante investigar las costumbres de la gente para dejar una buena impresión la primera vez.

Nuevo: Las vocales (The vowels)

El inglés no es un idioma fonético y por eso no se escribe siempre como suena. Tienes que aprender que las vocales pueden tener varios sonidos y aprender a pronunciar las palabras, una palabra a la vez.

En inglés, a diferencia del español, las vocales pueden producir sonidos distintos. Primero, vamos a aprender a pronunciar las vocales como las pronunciaríamos en el alfabeto:

- A – Se pronuncia como la E en ¡Epa!
- E – Se pronuncia como la I en Idea
- I – Se pronuncia como la palabra Hay
- O – Se pronuncia como la O en Oso
- U – Se pronuncia como IU, un sonido nuevo para el hispanohablante.

A

| Ape | Cake | Face |

E

Bee

Eel

Feet

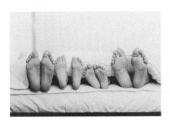

I

Bike

Kite

Pie

O

Coke

Rose

No

U

Mule

Used

You

Nuevo: Presentarnos/Introducing ourselves

- Hola. Me llamo _____.   Hi. My name is _____.
- ¿Cómo te llamas?   What is your name?
  - Me llamo _____.   My name is _____.

- ¡Mucho gusto!   It's Nice to meet you!
  - ¡Igualmente!   Likewise!

Lo de arriba es la manera más fácil de saludar a alguien en inglés. También puede expandir la conversación con las siguientes preguntas:

- ¿De dónde eres?   Where are you from?
  - Soy de _____.   I am from _____.
- ¿Dónde vives?   Where do you live?
  - Vivo en _____.   I live in _____.
- ¿Dónde trabajas?   Where do you work?
  - Trabajo en _____.   I work in _____.

Típicamente, a los hablantes de inglés les gusta hablar de cosas que disfrutan cuando se conocen por la primera vez.

Aquí hay unas ideas para comenzar:

¿Qué te gusta?	**What do you like?**
Me gusta _____.	**I like _____.**
No, no me gusta _____.	**No, I don't like _____.**

¡Practiquemos! Let's practice!

1. Do you like American food?   _____
2. Do you like Mexican food?   _____
3. Do you like Italian food?   _____
4. Do you like beer?   _____
5. Do you like wine?   _____
6. Do you like cocktails?   _____
7. Do you like soccer?   _____
8. Do you like football?   _____
9. Do you like baseball?   _____
10. Do you like to study?   _____
11. Do you like to cook?   _____
12. Do you like to dance?   _____

Nuevo: Preguntas útiles/Useful questions

English	Español
How do you say "libro"?	¿Cómo se dice libro?
What does "pencil" mean?	¿Qué significa pencil?
Can I ask a question?	¿Puedo hacer una pregunta?

Let's practice! Escriban las repuestas:

1. What does computer mean? _____
2. What does office mean? _____
3. What does paper mean? _____
4. What does empleado mean? _____
5. What does director mean? _____
6. What does student mean? _____
7. What does conference room mean? _____
8. What does classroom mean? _____

1. How do you say computadora? _____
2. How do you say oficina? _____
3. How do you say papel? _____
4. How do you say empleado? _____
5. How do you say director? _____
6. How do you say estudiante? _____
7. How do you say salón de conferencia? _____
8. How do you say salón de clase? _____

New: Cognates - Cognados

What does bank mean? ¡Que fácil! Bank means banco. Banco es un cognado. Los cognados son palabras en dos lenguas o más, que han surgido de una lengua en común.

Banca (Italian) ⟶ Banco (Spanish) ⟶ Banque (French) ⟶ Bank (English)

El primer banco en el mundo fue fundado en Italia en 1472. El sistema que apoyaba al comercio de Roma fue a Francia, dónde por el cambio de dialecto el nombre se convirtió en banque. Como los ingleses solían usar este sistema en esa época, "robaron" esta palabra "banque" de los franceses y es así que el primer "**bank**" nació.

Por lo tanto, nuestros idiomas no son tan distintos. Los dos idiomas son principalmente basados en el latín, por eso se escriben y suenan parecidamente. ¡Cuando tienes una duda, puedes adivinar!

Let's practice!

¿Qué significa _____?

Actor	_____	Hotel	_____
Chocolate	_____	Mango	_____
Director	_____	Normal	_____
Final	_____	Pasta	_____
		Simple	_____

Televisión _____

Nuevo: Números/Numbers (0 – 12)

0 –Zero	5 – Five	10 – Ten
1 – One	6 – Six	11 – Eleven
2 – Two	7 – Seven	12 – Twelve
3 – Three	8 – Eight	
4 – Four	9 – Nine	

Let's practice!

¿Cuánto cuesta …?   How much does a _____ cost?

Ejemplo: How much does a whiteboard cost?   <u>It costs 10 dollars.</u>

  9. How much does a piece of paper cost?   _____
10. How much does the pen cost?   _____
11. How much does a pencil cost?   _____
12. How much does a marker cost?   _____
13. How much does a package of paper cost   _____
14. How much does a box of pencils cost?   _____
15. How much does a box of pens cost?   _____
16. How much does a box of markers cost?   _____
17. How much does the English book cost?   _____
18. How much does the whiteboard cost?   _____

Nuevo: Despedidas/Saying goodbye

Let's stay in touch!

¡Estamos en contacto!

Until later!

Sounds good.

Me parece bien.

See you!

Kill two birds with one stone.
Matar dos pájaros de un tiro.

Nuevo: Vocabulario:

Español para la escuela y el trabajo

Cosas	Lugares	Personas
Computadora - Computer	Salón de conferencia – Conference Room	Profesor/Profesora - Teacher
Impresora - Printer	Salón de clase - Classroom	Estudiante - Student
Televisión - Television	Oficina - Office	Director/Directora - Director
Proyector - Projector	Escuela - School	Empleado/Empleada - Employee
Marcador - Marker		
Papel - Paper		

Flashcards (Tarjetas para memorizar)

En las páginas siguientes hemos puesto Flashcards. Estos son muy útiles para ayudarle a aprender inglés y memorizar el vocabulario nuevo. Antes de hacer la tarea, hay que primero memorizar el vocabulario. Memorizándolo podemos, por lo menos, entender el contexto de una conversación.

Así es como se usa la Flashcard:

1.) Ponga las flashcards en sus manos para que vea el lado escrito en inglés.

2.) Repásela diciendo la palabra en inglés en voz alta.

3.) Diga en voz alta lo que significa en español.

4.) Si lo dijo bien, póngala en un lado. Si lo dijiste mal, ponla con las otras que no has sabido su significado.

5.) Haga este ejercicio hasta que puedas saber el significado de todas las palabras correctamente.

6.) Ahora haga lo mismo, pero al revés (ve el lado escrito en español y diga la palabra en inglés).

Extra: ¡Intenta deletrearlas también!

Si hace este ejercicio antes de dormir y al momento de despertar, va a memorizarlas rapidísimo y va a poder usar el vocabulario nuevo inmediatamente.

Book

Pencil

Things

People

Paper

Teacher

Marker

Whiteboard

Student

Pen

Lápiz   Libro

Personas   Cosas

Profesor | Profesora   Papel

Pizarra   Marcador

Bolígrafo   Estudiante

How are you?   Hello

Goodbye   Good

Thanks   Kill two birds with one
                                stone.

Classroom   Conference Room

Printer   English

Hola

¿Cómo estás?

Bien

Adiós

Matar dos pájaros de un tiro.

Gracias

Salón de conferencia

Salón de clase

Inglés

Impresora

My name is

What is your name?

What does <u>palabra</u> mean?

How do you say <u>palabra</u>
in Spanish?

Where are you from?

Can I ask a question?

Let's stay in touch.

I am from

It costs

How much does _____
cost?

¿Cómo te llamas?

Me llamo

¿Cómo se dice palabra en español?

¿Qué significa palabra?

¿Puedo hacer una pregunta?

¿De dónde eres?

Soy de

Estamos en contacto.

¿Cuánto cuesta _____?

Cuesta

Computer

Sounds good.

Until later!

See you!

Director

Employee

Television

Projector

Office

Places

Me parece bien.

Computadora

¡Nos vemos!

¡Hasta luego!

Empleado | Empleada

Director | Directora

Proyector

Televisión

Lugares

Oficina

I like

What do you like?

It's nice to meet you!

Likewise

0 | 10

What is your phone number?

1 | 2 | 3

4 | 5 | 6

7 | 8 | 9

Where do you work?

¿Qué te gusta?   Me gusta

Igualmente   ¡Mucho gusto!

¿Cuál es tu número de   cero | diez
teléfono?

cuatro | cinco | seis   uno | dos | tres

¿Dónde trabajas?   siete | ocho | nueve

Activity – Conversation Skills

Si tiene un amigo quien habla inglés, practique este diálogo. También, si se encuentra solo, puede rellenar los espacios en blanco.

- Hello! How are you?
    - Hello I am _____.

    - My name is David. What is your name?
        - My name is _____.

    - Nice to meet you!
        - _____.

    - Where are you from?
        - I am from _____.

    - Where do you live?
        - I live in _____.

    - Where do you work?
        - I work in _____.

    - What do you like?
        - I like _____.

    - What is your telephone number?
        - _____

    - Let's stay in touch.
        - _____

    - Until later!

Lesson 2

Lesson Highlights

Review - Repaso
- Vowels
- Numbers
- Greetings

New
- Vocabulary and pronunciation
- Articles – A vs. an
- Shopping
- Colors
- I like
- Adjectives

Repaso (Review): The vowels

Recuerda, el inglés no es un idioma fonético y por eso no se escribe siempre como suena. Tienes que aprender que las vocales pueden tener varios sonidos y aprender a pronunciar las palabras, una palabra a la vez.

Largo Versus Corto Cuando una vocal suena como su nombre, se llama un sonido largo. Una vocal con el sonido corto produce otro sonido distinto y no es tan exagerado.	Vocal	El sonido largo	El sonido corto
	A	Apron	Apple
	E	Easel	Egg
	I	Ice cream	Iguana
	O	Overall	October
	U	University	Umbrella

New: Practicando inglés

Consulte la sección "Consejos de estudio para aprender a hablar inglés" de este libro en la página 13 para obtener más información sobre esta actividad. El segundo consejo es practicar hablar inglés. En pocas palabras, si desea comenzar a hablar inglés con confianza, aprenda esta frase y úsela cada vez que escuche a alguien hablar inglés:

- Hi! My name is _____. I'm learning English. Can we practice?
  - Yes, of course!

Repaso: Presentándonos

1. Hi! My name is David. I'm learning English. Can we practice?
   _____
2. What is your name?
   _____
3. Nice to meet you!
   _____

4. Where are you from?

_____

5. Where do you live?

_____

6. Where do you work?

_____

7. What do you like?

_____

8. What is your telephone number?

_____

9. Let's stay in touch!

_____

10. See you later!

_____

Nuevo: La Charla Trivial (Small Talk)

Igual que en español, hay que saber charlar de cosas triviales, lo que llamamos small talk in inglés:

1. En el trabajo
2. En la comunidad
3. Durantes sus viajes

¡La palabra "LIKE" nos da posibilidades infinitas!

Do you like to go to _____?
- The movies
- The theater
- Museums
- Concerts

Do you like to listen to _____?
- Music
- The radio
- The news

Do you like to take _____?
- Pictures
- English classes

Do you like to drink _____?
- Café
- Cerveza

Do you like to _____?
- Ski
- *Snowboard*
- Play sports

Repaso: Vocabulario

1. How do you say lápiz in English?   _____
2. How do you say bolígrafo in English?   _____
3. How do you say libro in English?   _____
4. How do you say papel in English   _____
5. How do you say marcador in English?   _____
6. How do you say pizarra in English?   _____
7. How do you say maestro in English?   _____
8. How do you say estudiante in English   _____
9. How much does a pencil cost?   _____
10. How much does a pen cost?   _____
11. How much does a book cost?   _____
12. How much does a pack of paper cost?   _____
13. How much does a marker cost?   _____
14. How much does a whiteboard cost?   _____

Nuevo: Consejo para aprender inglés – Relevancia

Cuando estás aprendiendo cómo hablar otro idioma ¡tiene que hacerlo relevante!
Piense en tres cosas en su oficina o escuela que quiere saber cómo decir. Practique con alguien que hable inglés o use un dicciónario Inglés/Español para buscar estas palabras.

* How do you say _____? You say _____.
* How do you say _____? You say _____.
* How do you say _____? You say _____.

New: Masculine/Feminine

Una diferencia importante entre inglés y español es que no todas las palabras pueden ser masculinas o femeninas. Solo personas y animales tienen género. Vamos a aplicar este concepto a las personas primero.

La mayoría de las palabras no son iguales y cambian mucho dependiendo del sexo de la persona:

Masculine	Feminine
Niño – Boy	Niña - Girl

Los artículos son palabras que nos ayudan a definir de lo que estamos hablando. Por ejemplo, EL y LA son artículos. En inglés, es la misma palabra y no cambia dependiendo del género de la persona de quien se está hablando:

* El/La – The (masculino y femenino)

Hay un par de cosas que necesitamos aprender para hablar inglés bien:

1.) Las palabras para describir personas masculinas y femeninas normalmente cambian, pero los artículos son iguales:

- The boy/The girl
-

2.) Las profesiones en EEUU legalmente tienen que ser iguales para hombres y mujeres:
  - El profesor/La Profesora - The professor
  - El patrón/La patrona   - The boss

3.) Finalmente, los títulos familiares normalmente cambian:

- Uncle (Tío)   Aunt (Tía)

Nuevo: Plural

Otra cosa fácil del inglés es que el artículo THE es igual en la forma singular y plural:

- Los/Las – The

Para hacer los sustantivos plurales, tenemos un par de cosas que aprender:

1.) Agrega S a la mayoría de las palabras, igual que en español:

- The boy/The boys
- The girl/The girls

2.) Agrega ES a sustantivos que terminan con el sonido de S. Pueden terminar con las letras S, X, Z, CH, o SH:

- The boss/The bosses
- The box/The boxes

3.) Grupos con géneros mezclados pueden resultar en una palabra distinta:

- The boys + The girls = the children

Gender	Singular	Plural
Masculino	The father	The fathers
Femenino	The mother	The mothers

De nuevo, combinando los dos géneros, obtenemos la palabra *PARENTS* por padres.

Let's practice! Rellena los espacios en blanco con el artículo correcto. Después convierta al plural.

Singular	Plural
1. _____ brother	_____
2. _____ sister	_____
3. _____ brother + _____ sister =	_____
4. _____ mother	_____
5. _____ father	_____
6. _____ mother + _____ father =	_____
7. _____ student	_____
8. _____ teacher	_____
9. _____ man	_____
10. _____ woman	_____
11. _____ man + _____ woman =	_____
12. _____ professor	_____
13. _____ son	_____
14. _____ daughter	_____
15. _____ son + _____ daughter =	_____

New: Las cosas son neutrales

En este aspecto el inglés es más fácil, porque el concepto de masculino y femenino solo aplica a personas y no a cosas. Las cosas son neutrales en inglés.

Masculine	Feminine	Neutral
El libro	La mesa	The book, The table

Las reglas de arriba valen aquí también:

1.) Agregue **S** a la mayoría de las palabras e **ES** a las palabras que terminan con S, X, Z, CH, o SH:

- The book/The books
- The table/The tables
- The class/The classes

Otra reglita aquí – las palabras que terminan con Y tienen dos cambios posibles:

Si una vocal viene antes, simplemente se agrega S:

- The boy/The boys

Si un consonante viene antes:

- Cambie la Y por la I
- Agregue ES

Ejemplo: The candy/The candies

Let's practice! Complete el espacio en blanco con el artículo correcto para la palabra correspondiente. Luego cámbialo a la forma plural.

1. _____ pencil   _____
2. _____ paper   _____
3. _____ book   _____
4. _____ pen   _____
5. _____ whiteboard   _____
6. _____ class   _____
7. _____ chair   _____
8. _____ marker   _____
9. _____ candy   _____
10. _____ backpack   _____

New: Las compras - Shopping

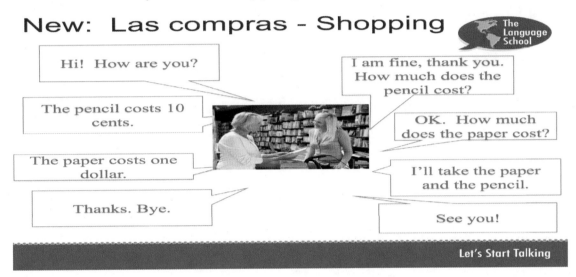

New: Las compras - Shopping

The Language School

Hi! How are you?

I am fine, thank you. How much does the pencil cost?

The pencil costs 10 cents.

OK. How much does the paper cost?

The paper costs one dollar.

I'll take the paper and the pencil.

Thanks. Bye.

See you!

Let's Start Talking

Let's practice! Rellene los espacios en blanco basado en esta información:

1.) You need to buy (usted necesita comprar):

- **El lápiz ($0.10)**
- **El libro ($9)**

Hi! How are you?

_____ _____ fine, thank you. How much does _____ _____ cost?

_____ _____ costs _____ _____.

Ok. How much does _____ _____ cost?

_____ _____ costs _____ _____.

I will take _____ _____ and _____ _____.

Thanks! Bye.

_____ _____!

2.) You need to buy

- **Un bolígrafo ($1)**
- **Un paquete de papel ($2)**

Hi! How are you?

_____ _____ fine, thank you. How much does _____

_____ cost?

_____ _____ costs _____ _____.

Ok. How much does _____ _____ cost?

_____ _____ costs _____ _____.

I will take _____ _____ and _____ _____.

Thanks! Bye.

_____ _____!

3.) You need to buy

- **Un marcador ($3)**
- **Una pizarra ($10)**

Hi! How are you?

_____ _____ fine, thank you. How much does _____

_____ cost?

_____ _____ costs _____ _____.

Ok. How much does _____ _____ cost?

_____ _____ costs _____ _____.

I will take _____ _____ and _____ _____.

Thanks! Bye.

_____ _____!

Repaso: Los números

Vamos a repasar los números. Pero primero, vamos aprender dos frases nuevas:

Hay

There are (plural):	There are 3 pencils.	(Hay 3 lápices.)
There is (singular):	There is 1 blue pencil.	(Hay un lápiz azul.)

1. How many books are there?   There are _____ _____.
2. How many pens are there?   There are _____ _____.
3. How many whiteboards are there?   There are _____ _____.

4. How many pencils are there?

There are _____ _____.

5. How many markers are there?   There are _____ _____.
6. How many plants are there?   There are _____ _____.

7. How many students are there?   There are _____ _____.
8. How many teachers are there?   There is _____ _____.

New: Pronunciation - TH

El inglés tiene varios sonidos que no existen en español. Uno de ellos es el sonido producido por la combinación de la T y la H, o sea, TH. La TH en inglés produce un ceceo. Por ejemplo, para hablar del número 3 en inglés se dice:

- **Three**   **Three debería ser pronunciado THree.**

Hispanohablantes pueden decir *Tree*, lo que significa árbol. Vamos a aprender pronunciarlo bien.

Primero que nada, si quiere pronunciar la TH, usted puede. ¡Piense positivamente! Dígase "sí se puede" y siga practicando hasta que lo pueda hacer. Una parte grande de aprender idiomas nuevos es psicológica, y si usted es positivo y sigue intentando, eventualmente podrá hacerlo. Igualmente, si se dice que no puede, nunca podrá hacerlo. Entonces ¡piense positivamente y siga intentando!

Pues, ¿cómo se puede pronunciar la TH?

Hay que mover la lengua a la frente de la boca y presionarla a los puntos de los dientes de arriba. ¿Puedes sentir dónde está la lengua? Ahí es donde tiene que estar para empezar a producir este sonido.

Después, simplemente empujas aire por la boca, manteniendo la lengua en contacto con los dientes.

Este sonido va a ser más fácil para la gente de España. Si usted no es de España, ¿ha oído un español pronunciar la palabra cerveza? Se la dice con un ceceo:

Cerveza – Thervetha

Let's practice:

1. That	5. These	9. Thursday
2. Thanks	6. Thin	10. Thunder
3. The	7. This	
4. Theater	8. Those	

New: Possessive Adjectives

What is **your** name?
My name is David.

> Your = Tu
> My - Mi

En este saludo vemos las palabras MY y YOUR, que son adjetivos posesivos.
What is your name?

Nuevo: Los colores

Pink	Grey	Black
Blue	White	Yellow
Orange	Red	Purple
Brown		Green

Let's practice!

1.	What color is the pencil?	The pencil is _____(Amarillo)
2.	What color is the door?	The door is _____. (Marron)
3.	What color is the book?	The book is _____. (Rojo)
4.	What color is the window?	The window is _____ (Blanco)
5.	What color is the table?	The table is _____. (Marrón)
6.	What color is the whiteboard?	The whiteboard is _____. (Blanco)
7.	What color is the plant?	The plant is _____. (Verde)
8.	What color is the chair?	The chair is _____. (Negro)
9.	What color is the marker?	The marker is _____ (Anaranjado)
10.	What color is the telephone?	The telephone is _____(Negro).
11.	What color is the dog?	The dog is _____. (Gris)
12.	What color is the rose?	The rose is _____. (Rosado)

New: I like /You like (Me gusta/Te gusta)

Un buen tema de conversación para hacer amigos nuevos es hablar de lo que le gusta.

Para decir que le gusta algo, diga "I like" seguido por lo que le gusta:

- I like English.
- I like soccer.
- I like Mexican food.

*Fíjese que en inglés no se usa el artículo.

You like significa "te gusta":

- You like English.
- You like soccer.
- You like Mexican food.

Para preguntar hay un cambio en la estructura y vamos a empezar con la palabra DO, lo que siempre se usa para preguntar en inglés:

Do you like soccer?

*Fíjese que en inglés no se usa la marca de interrogación "¿" para empezar las preguntas.

Para contestar de la manera más completa, puedes decir lo siguiente:

- Yes, I like soccer.
- No, I don't like soccer.

1. Do you like pizza?

_____.

2. Do you like tigers?

_____.

3. Do you like the movie *Casablanca*?

_____.

4. Do you like beer?

_____.

5. Do you prefer beer or wine?

_____.

6. Do you like the beach?

_____.

7. Do you like the guitar?

_____.

8. Do you like snow?

_____.

9. Do you like Colorado?

_____.

10. Do you like Mexican food?

_____.

Nuevo: Agregando detalle

Al igual que hablar de cosas que te gustan, cuando conoces gente nueva, ¡también puedes contarles tus cosas favoritas! Veamos un ejemplo:

What is your favorite sport?

- Soccer is my favorite.
- I like soccer.

Fíjese que puede responder diciendo qué deporte es su favorito, o simplemente si le gusta el fútbol.

1. What is your favorite food?
(American food | Mexican food | Italian food | Cuban food)

_____.

2. What is your favorite animal?
(dog | cat | horse | fish | bird | whale | dolphin | tiger | lion)

_____.

3. What is your favorite movie genre?
(horror | comedy | romance | adventure | action | suspense | fantasy)

_____.

4. What is your favorite drink?
(juice | soda | beer | wine | drink | water | coffee | tea | milk)

_____.

   4. What is your favorite state?
   5.
(Colorado | New York | California | Florida | Washington | Wyoming | Arizona | Nevada)

_____.

6. What is your favorite dish?
(steak with salad | Meatloaf | Chicken enchiladas | Lasagna | Seafood)

_____.

7. What is your favorite sport?
(Baseball | Soccer | American football | Basketball | Hockey | Rugby | Volleyball)

_____.

8. What is your favorite place?
(beach | mountains | city | countryside | house | park | club | downtown)

_____.

9. What is your favorite instrument?
(guitar | piano | bass | drums | percussion | saxophone | violin | banjo)

_____.

10. What is your favorite weather?
(Hot | cold | rainy | snowy | tropical | humid | dry| warm)

_____.

Nuevo: Más despedidas

Nuevo Vocabulario: Adjetivos (Adjectives)

Grande/Big   Pequeño/Little
Bonito/Beautiful   Feo/Ugly
Nuevo/New   Viejo/Old
Caro/Expensive   Barato/Cheap
Rico/Rich   Pobre/Poor
Bueno/Good   Malo/Bad

Big   Little

Good   Bad

New   Old

Expensive   Cheap

Ugly   Beautiful

Pequeño	Grande
Malo	Bueno
Viejo	Nuevo
Barato	Caro
Bonito	Feo

Your   My

His

Her   There is/There are

Grey   The

Name   Bye

Red   Blue

Mi

Tu

Hay

Su

El, La, Los, Las

Gris

Chao, Adiós

Nombre

Azul

Rojo

Brown   Purple

Black   White

Green   Orange

Yellow   Pink

I like   I don't like

Morado

Marrón

Blanco

Negro

Anaranjado

Verde

Rosado

Amarillo

No me gusta

Me gusta

Lesson 3

Lesson Highlights

Review

- My pleasures/preferences
- Shopping
- Indefinite articles
- Colors

New

- More Greetings and goodbyes
- Adjectives
- Conversation – In your opinion…

New: Greetings

En inglés hay muchas maneras de saludar la gente: What's up? =¿Qué pasa?

Hey! What's up?

- Nothing much.
- It's all good.
- Chilling.

- Buenos días (Good morning)
- Buenas tardes (Good afternoon)
- Buenas noches (Good evening/good night)

Dependiendo de la hora del día, hay saludos específicos que puede usar.

New: Goodbyes

- Goodbye (Adiós)
No es una regla, pero "goodbye" normalmente se considera como un adiós "fuerte".

- See you tomorrow!
- Take care!
- Later!
- Have a nice day!

Estas despedidas son muy comunes.

¡Practiquemos!

¿Qué diría usted en estas situaciones?

1. Llega a la escuela a las 10:30 AM y ve a sus compañeros o a su maestro.

   _____

2. Está saliendo de su trabajo, pero va a ver a sus colegas mañana.

   _____

3. Se está econtrando con unos amigos para almorzar a la 1 PM.

   _____

4. Se está encontrando con unos amigos para tomar tragos a las 10 PM.

   _____

5. Se está yendo del bar a las 11 PM para volver a casa.

   _____

6. Acaba de terminar un semestre en el extranjero en EEUU y está volviendo a México.

   _____

7. La clase se acabó. Va a ver a sus compañeros la próxima semana.

   _____

8. Está regresando a casa para prepararse para salir por la noche con sus compañeros.

   _____

Review: Introductions

Contesta a las siguientes preguntas con oraciones completas:

1. Hi! My name is _____. I am studying English. Can we practice?

   _____

2. What is your name?

   _____

3. Nice to meet you!

   _____

4. Where are you from?

   _____

5. Where do you live?

   _____

6. Where do you work?

   _____

7. What do you like?

   _____

8. What is your telephone number?

   _____

9. Let's stay in touch.

   _____

10. See you later.

   _____

New: Useful phrases

Cuando aprende un idioma nuevo, es importante admitir cuando no entiende algo. ¡La gente intentará ayudarle a entender! Con las siguientes frases y con las tres preguntas que aprendieron en la lección 1, debería de poder llegar a entender en prácticamente cada situación en la que se encuentra.

English	Español
I don't understand.	No entiendo.
Please, repeat!	¡Repite, por favor!
Slower, please!	¡Más despacio por favor!

Let's practice!

¿Qué dirías si alguien vino a usted y le dijo lo siguiente?
Oh beautiful, for spacious skies, for amber waves of grain
For purple mountain majesties above the fruited plain
America, America, God shed his grace on thee

1. _____
2. _____
3. _____
4. _____
5. _____
6. _____

New: Ray Charles/Escuchar

Parte de aprender como hablar inglés es aprender escucharlo. Somos afortunados de vivir durante un tiempo cuando puedes buscar canciones en YouTube y la letra en línea para ayudarle practicar. Comenzaremos con el legendario Ray Charles, uno de los personajes más influyentes y más queridos de la música estadounidense "soul".

Escuche esta canción en YouTube con el enlace abajo y siga la letra, o "lyrics", en la página siguiente.

https://www.youtube.com/watch?v=5yaetvTj5DE

Ray Charles - America The Beautiful

Qué hermoso que los héroes probaron durante la lucha liberadora Quienes amaron más a nuestro país que a sí mismos y la misericordia más que la vida	Oh beautiful for heroes proved in liberating strife Who more than self our country loved, and mercy more than life
América, América, que Dios refine tu oro	America, America, may God thy gold refine
Hasta que el éxito sea la nobleza y cada ganancia sea divina	Till all success be nobleness and every gain divine
Y tú sabes, cuando estaba en la escuela solíamos cantar algo así, escucha aquí:	And you know when I was in school we used to sing it something like this, listen here:
Qué hermosa, por los cielos espaciosos, por las olas ambarinas de grano	Oh beautiful, for spacious skies, for amber waves of grain
Por las majestades de las montañas moradas encima de los planos fértiles	For purple mountain majesties above the fruited plain
Pero espera un minuto, estoy hablando de América, dulce América	But now wait a minute, I'm talking about America, sweet America
Tú sabes, Dios derramó su gracia en ti	You know, God done shed his grace on thee
Te coronó bien, sí lo hizo, en una hermandad, de un mar a otro mar brillante	He crowned thy good, yes, he did, in a brotherhood, from sea to shining sea
Sabes, ojalá tuviera quién me ayudara a cantar esto	You know, I wish I had somebody to help me sing this
Coro: América, América, Dios derramó su gracia en ti **Ray**: América, te quiero América, lo ves	**Chorus:** America, America, God shed his grace on thee **Ray:** America, I love you America, you see
Dios mío derramó su gracia en ti y lo debería de querer por eso	My God he done shed his grace on thee, And you ought a love him for it, Cause
Porque Él, Él, Él te coronó bien, y me dijo que lo haría, con hermandad	He, He, He, crowned thy good, He told me he would, with brotherhood
Coro: De un mar a otro mar brillante **Ray**: Oh señor, o señor, te agradezco señor	**Chorus**: From sea to shining sea **Ray:** Oh Lord, oh Lord, I thank you Lord

Conversation:

- What's your favorite music? _____
- Do you like Ray Charles' music? _____

New: Pronunciation - Y y LL

En inglés la Y produce un sonido similar:

Yard - Hiard
Yellow - Hielo
Yikes - Hiayks

You - Hiu
Yummy – Hiamy

En inglés, la LL produce un sonido similar a la L:

Bully – Buli
Chilly – Chili
Cell – Cel

Really – Rily
Wallet - Walet

Review: Classroom

How do you say _____?

1. Lápiz _____
2. Bolígrafo _____
3. Marcador _____
4. Libro _____
5. Papel _____
6. Pizarra _____

7. El cuaderno _____
8. La cinta adhesiva _____
9. El borrador _____
10. La tarjetas de negocio _____
11. La tijeras _____
12. Las carpetas. _____

Review: Shopping

Let's practice! Rellene los espacios en blanco.

1.) You need to buy the pencil and the book.
Hello   How are you?
_____ _____, thank you. How much _____ _____
_____ _____?
_____ _____ costs _____ _____.
Ok. How much _____ _____ _____ _____?
_____ _____ costs _____ _____.
I will take_____ _____ and _____ _____.

2.) You need to buy the pen and the pack of paper.
Hello   How are you?
_____ _____, thank you. How much _____ _____
_____ _____?
_____ _____ costs _____ _____.
Ok. How much _____ _____ _____ _____?
_____ _____ costs _____ _____.
I will take_____ _____ and _____ _____.

3.) You need to buy the marker and the whiteboard:

Hello How are you?

_____ _____ _____ , thank you. How much _____ _____
_____ _____ ?
_____ _____ costs _____ _____ .
Ok. How much _____ _____ _____ _____ ?
_____ _____ costs _____ _____ .
I will take_____ _____ and _____ _____ .

Nuevo: Artículos indefinidos

Antes, aprendemos del artículo definido EL/LA/LOS/LAS (THE). Se llama artículo definido porque cuando lo usamos estamos definiendo precisamente de lo que estamos hablando.
Por ejemplo, si yo dijera "páseme el marcador verde", usted sabría cuál marcador verde pasarme, porque es el único marcador verde que ve.

Si yo dijera "páseme un marcador", es posible que me preguntaría de qué color o simplemente me pasaría cualquiera de los marcadores que ve, porque no he definido un marcador específico que deseo.

Un/Una es un artículo indefinido. Vamos a aprender cómo hacerlo en inglés.

Como la mayoría de las palabras son neutrales en inglés, los artículos no dependen de eso, sino del tipo de letra con la que empieza la palabra. Aquí lo que vale es si la letra es consonante o vocal:

A: Viene antes de palabras que empiezan con consonante	An: Viene antes de palabras que empiezan con vocal	Some: Viene antes de palabras plurales, no importa la primera letra
Un Niño – **A Boy** Una Niña – **A Girl**	Un premio – An award Una Manzana – **An** apple	Some boys Some girls Some apples Some awards

Recuerde usar las mismas reglas de antes para hacer los sustantivos plurales:

1.) Agrega S a la mayoría de las palabras

- A boy/Some boys
- A girl/Some girls

2.) Agrega ES a las palabras que terminan con S, X, Z, CH, o SH:

- The class/The classes

3.) Grupos con géneros mezclados puede resultar en una palabra nueva:

- Some boys + Some girls = Some children

60

Let's practice! Rellene con el artículo correcto según la palabra. Después cámbielo a plural.

	Singular		Plural

Singular   **Plural**

1. _____ brother   _____
2. _____ sister   _____
3. _____ brother + _____ sister =   _____
4. _____ mother   _____
5. _____ father   _____
6. _____ mother + _____ father =   _____
7. _____ student   _____
8. _____ teacher   _____
9. _____ aunt   _____
10. _____ uncle   _____
11. _____ aunt + _____ uncle =   _____
12. _____ boss   _____
13. _____ son   _____
14. _____ daughter   _____
15. _____ son + _____ daughter =   _____

Don't forget to apply this rule to things as well!

Let's practice! Fill in the correct article for the corresponding word. Then change to plural.

1. _____ pencil   _____
2. _____ apple   _____
3. _____ book   _____
4. _____ orange   _____
5. _____ whiteboard _____
6. _____ eraser   _____
7. _____ chair   _____
8. _____ idea   _____
9. _____ umbrella   _____
10. _____ backpack   _____

Nuevo: Las compras – La Segunda Parte

Let's apply this to real life:

Hello! How are you?

Fine, thank you. I need a pencil. How much is it?

A pencil costs 10 cents.

Ok. I need an eraser too.

An eraser costs 10 dollars.

I will take the pencil and the eraser.

Thank you. Bye.

See you later!

Necesito – I need
También – too/also

Inicialmente usamos el artículo indefinido a/an (un/una) para pedir algo.
Después de decidir <u>cual</u> queremos, cambiamos al artículo definido the (el/la).

Let's Start Talking

Nuevo: Las compras – Segunda parte

Let's practice! Rellene los espacios según esta información:

1.) You need to buy a pencil and a book.

Hello   How are you?
Fine, thank you. I need ___ _____. How much is it?

_____ _____ costs _____ _____.
Ok. I need ___ _____ too.

_____ _____ costs _____ _____.
I will take _____ _____ and _____ _____.

Thank you. Bye!
_____ _____ _____!

2.) You need to buy a pen and a pack of paper.

Hello   How are you?
Fine, thank you. I need ___ _____. How much is it?

_____ _____ costs _____ _____.
Ok. I need ___ _____ ___ _____ too.

_____ _____ costs _____ _____.
I will take _____ _____ and _____ _____.

Thank you. Bye!
_____ _____ _____!

3.) You need to buy an apple and an orange.

Hello   How are you?
Fine, thank you. I need ___ _____. How much is it?

_____ _____ costs _____ _____.
Ok. I need ___ _____ too.

_____ _____ costs _____ _____.
I will take _____ _____ and _____ _____.

Thank you. Bye!
_____ _____ _____!

Review: I like

1. Do you like motorcycles?
   _____.
2. Do you prefer a car or motorcycle?
   I prefer _____.
3. Do you like the summer?
   _____.
4. What season do you prefer?
   I prefer _____.
5. Do you like Rock music?
   _____.
6. What kind of music do you prefer?
   I prefer _____.
7. Do you like to read?
   _____.
8. What type of book do you like to read?
   I prefer _____.

Seasons of the year

Spring
Summer
Fall
Summer

Book Genres

Fiction
Non fiction
Drama
Comedy
Mystery
Science Fiction

New: I like things - Plural

Para hablar de las cosas que nos gustan se toma en cuenta que no hay cambio en el verbo. Se nota una diferencia en que en el inglés casi siempre se usa la forma plural sin el artículo:

I like – Singular/Plural

- Do you like English classes?   Yes, I like English classes.

Let's practice! Circle the most appropriate sentence

1. I like tigers.   I like the tigers.
2. I like the dogs.   I like dogs.
3. I like the cats.   I like cats.
4. I like birds.   I like the birds.
5. I like fish.   I like the fish.
6. I like the horses.   I like horses.
7. I like hamburgers.   I like the hamburgers.
8. I like the beer.   I like beer.
9. I like cocktails.   I like the cocktails.
10. I like the soda.   I like soda.

1. Do you like pizza?   _____
2. Do you like animals?   _____
3. Do you like funny movies?   _____
4. Do you like Ray Charles' music? _____
5. What is your favorite activity? _____
6. What is your favorite animal?   _____
7. What is your favorite country? _____

8. What is your favorite music? _____

Nuevo: Los adjetivos

Adjetivos son palabras descriptivas que nos ayudan formar oraciones completas y detalladas. Vamos a aprender usar los adjetivos para describir cosas en inglés.

1.) Los adjetivos son usados al revés que español.

En inglés, el adjetivo precede la palabra que describe.

- The tall man.

En español, viene después:

- El hombre alto (the man tall)

2.) Las personas y animales pueden ser masculinos o femeninos, pero los adjetivos y artículos siempre son neutrales
- The short boy
- The short girl

3.) Para hablar de varias cosas:
- Adjetivos nunca cambian por número.

Ejemplos	
Singular	Plural
• A tall boy • A tall girl	• Some tall boys • Some tall girls

Let's practice! Usa los adjetivos de la caja para describir las siguientes cosas. Después, cambia a la forma plural.

1.) A _____ dog.
2.) A _____ dog.
3.) _____.
4.) _____.

Big/Small
Beautiful/Ugly
New/Old
Expensive/Cheap
Rich/Poor
Good/Bad

5.) A _____ apple.
6.) A _____ apple.
7.) _____.
8.) _____.

9.) An _____ cat.
10.)A _____ cat.
11.)_____.
12.)_____.

13.)A _____ car.
14.)An _____ car.
15.)_____.
16.)_____.

17.)A _____ watch.
18.)An _____ watch.
19.)_____.
20.)_____.

21.)A _____ man.
22.)A _____ man.
23.)_____.
24.)_____.

25.)A _____ student
26.)A _____ student.
27.)_____.
28.)_____.

New: Conversation – In your opinion

Is the beach beautiful?

_____

Do you prefer the beach or the mountains?

_____

Are magazines expensive?

_____

What is your favorite magazine?

_____

Is beer good?

_____

Do you like beer or wine more?

_____

Is fast food bad?

_____

What kind of fast food do you dislike?

_____

Is the city of Denver old?

_____

What is your favorite city?

_____

Is Penelope Cruz ugly?

_____

Who is your favorite actor or actress?

_____

Are cartoons popular?

_____

Do you like cartoons?

_____

Is wine delicious?

_____

Do you like white wine or red wine?

_____

Nuevo: Vocabulario – Los verbos

Ordenar - Order

Tomar/Beber - Drink

Reservar - Reserve

Desear - Want

Comer - Eat

To order

To drink

To reserve

To want

To drink

To eat

It's all good

Excellent

Cool, tranquil

Good morning

Tomar   Ordenar

Desear   Reservar

Comer   Beber

Excelente   Todo bien

Buenos días   Tranquilo

Good afternoon   Good evening/Good night

Goodbye   Until tomorrow

See you later   Until later

Bye   A, An, Some

Man   Woman

Buenas noches   Buenas tardes

Hasta mañana   Adiós

Hasta luego   Nos vemos

Un, una
unos, unas   Chao

Mujer   Hombre

Apple

Banana

Blueberry

Strawberry

Orange

Lettuce

Green beans

Carrot

Cabbage

Red bell pepper

El plátano   La manzana

La fresa   El arándano

La lechuga   La naranja

La zanahoria   Las judías verdes

El pimiento rojo   La col

Lección 4

Lesson Highlights

Review
- Introductions
- Do you like?
- Articles, adjectives, and nouns

New
- Regular verbs
- How to order food
- Conversation: American food
- Reading: United States

Review: Introductions

¡Practica el siguiente diálogo con alguien que habla inglés!

1.) Hi. How are you?

    A. Very well, thanks
    B. I'm ok
    C. Not good
    D. Fine
    E. Excellent

And you?

2.) What is your name?
My name is _____.
And you?

3.) Nice to meet you.
    A. Likewise
    B. You too
    C. It's a pleasure.

4.) Where do you live?
I live in _____.
And you?

5.) Where are you from ?
I'm from _____.
And you?

6.) What do you do?
I am a _____.
And you?

7.) Where do you work?
I work _____.

¿Y tú? – And you?

Para ser verdaderamente conversacional, tiene que poder intercambiar preguntas y respuestas. Esto es una manera fácil de agregar a la conversación.

Preguntando sobre el trabajo
La manera correcta de preguntar "¿A qué te dedicas?" es decir:

"What do you do?"

Típicamente, respondes diciendo:

I am a + profesión
Soy _____

Si estás jubilado, se dice:
I am retired.

73

And you?

8.) Do you like to _____?

- Dance
- Cook
- Play soccer
- Ski
- Travel
- Drink wine
- Run
- Read
- Go shopping
- A. Yes, I like to _____.
- B. No, I do not like to _____.

9.) Goodbye.

- A. Until next time.
- B. See you later.
- C. Bye.

Repaso: Frases útiles

Imagínese que está en un restaurante de parilla americana con su maestro.

¿Que haría si el mesero le diera algo con lo siguiente escrito?

- How do you say____?
- What does _____ mean?
- Can I ask a question?
- I don't understand.
- Please, repeat.
- Slower, please!

Menu		
Appetizers	**Meats**	**Drinks**
Salad	Beef	Sparkling water
Maryland Crab cakes	Chicken	Red wine
French Fries	Pork	Cocktails

1. _____
2. _____
3. _____

El mesero vuelve a su mesa y le dice lo siguiente:

Good evening ladies and gentlemen, let me tell you about the special of the day. It is filet mignon wrapped in bacon along with mashed potatoes and a Caesar salad. I'll give you a minute to think, but in the meantime, would you like something to drink, like wine or a cocktail?

¿Qué le contestarías?

1. _____
2. _____
3. _____

New: American food

1. Do you like sodas? _____
2. Do you like juice? _____
3. Which do you prefer to drink? _____
1. Do you like whiskey? _____
2. Do you like beer? _____
3. Which do you prefer to drink? _____
1. Do you like French fries? _____
2. Do you like chicken wings? _____
3. Which do you prefer to order? _____
1. Do you like turkey sandwiches? _____
2. Do you like roast beef sandwiches? _____
3. Which do you prefer to eat? _____
1. Do you like chicken soup? _____
2. Do you like salad? _____
3. Which do you prefer to order? _____
1. Do you like barbeque? _____
2. Do you like grilled steak? _____
3. Which do you prefer to eat? _____
1. ¿Do you like hamburgers? _____
2. Do you like fried chicken? _____
3. Which do you prefer to order? _____
1. Do you like ice cream? _____
2. Do you like apple pie? _____
3. Which do you prefer to eat? _____

New: Fruits and vegetables

Llena los blancos con el artículo indefinido (A/AN/SOME) y un adjetivo y después contesta las preguntas.

1.) _____ apple is _____.
2.) _____ strawberry is _____.
3.) _____ bananas are _____.
4.) _____ blueberries are _____.
5.) _____ oranges are _____.

6.) _____ head of lettuce is _____.
7.) _____ green beans are _____.
8.) _____ carrot is _____.
9.) _____ head of red cabbage is _____.
10.)_____ red bell pepper is _____.
11.) Do you like apples? _____
12.) Do you like strawberries? _____
13.)Do you like bananas? _____
14.)Do you like blueberries? _____
15.)Do you like oranges? _____
16.)Do you like lettuce? _____
17.)Do you like green beans? _____
18.)Do you like carrots? _____
19.)Do you like cabbage? _____
20.)Do you like red bell peppers? _____

Review: The English Classroom

Escriba oraciones completas para describir las siguientes cosas en el salón de inglés. Use un adjetivo y un color para cada uno.

Adjectives	Colors
• Beautiful	• Orange
• Ugly	• Red
• New	• Green
• Old	• Yellow
• Big	• Blue
• Small	• Black
• Expensive	• Brown
• Cheap	• White
• Good	• Purple
• Bad	• Grey

Ex: The window is beautiful and white.

1.) Pencil _____
2.) Book _____
3.) Table _____
4.) Whiteboard _____
5.) Plant _____
6.) Chair _____
7.) Marker _____
8.) Pen _____
9.) Telephone _____
10.)Window _____

Repaso: Artículos, sustantivos y adjetivos

Mire los artículos, sustantivos y adjetivos en las siguientes oraciones, ¿están correctos?
Conteste: **CORRECT** or **INCORRECT**. Corrija los que son incorrectos.

1. The book is reds. _____
2. The plants are beautiful. _____
3. A telephones are white. _____
4. The whiteboard is bigs. _____
5. Some house are cheaps. _____
6. A elephant is bad. _____
7. The restaurant is small. _____
8. A doctors are good. _____
9. An beach is ugly. _____
10. A actress is beautiful. _____

Describe your ...
1. Car _____
2. House _____
3. Computer _____
4. Clothes _____
5. Favorite flower _____
6. Television _____
7. Favorito color _____
8. National flag _____

New: Verbs

Para poder conversar en inglés, aprender a conjugar los verbos es necesario. Vamos a comenzar trabajando con los verbos.

Primero, ¿qué es un verbo? Un verbo es tipo de palabra que expresa acción.
Ejemplo:

- I eat burritos.   Yo como burritos.

En este ejemplo **comer** es el verbo. Si tiene dudas, puede preguntarse qué está pasando y identificarás el verbo.

En inglés, el verbo no cambia tanto como en español, pero el sujeto sí cambia dependiendo de quién está haciendo la acción.

1. Yo como burritos.   I eat burritos.
2. Tú comes burritos.   You eat burritos.

Usted puede ver en este ejemplo que en español los verbos cambian mucho. La forma del verbo *comer* cambia con el sujeto, y por eso es yo como y tú comes. En inglés el verbo no cambia pero el sujeto sí:

I eat/You eat

Con los verbos regulares, hay dos cambios verbales y tres cambios de la estructura posible en el presente simple en inglés, dependiendo de quién o qué está haciendo la acción y si la oración es negativa, positiva, o interrogativa. Sin embargo, en esta etapa de su carrera en inglés, solo es importante saber un cambio verbal y los tres cambios de la estructura para llegar a conversar, como la mayoría de las conversaciones involucrarán:

1. La gente preguntándole   TÚ   DO YOU + VERBO
2. Usted contestando las preguntas   YO   I + VERBO

    Ejemplo: ¿Tú comes hamburguesas?   Do you eat hamburgers?
                     Sí, yo como hamburguesas.   Yes, I eat hamburgers.

Lo más importante es aprender la estructura de las oraciones:

- **Positivas**   - **Negativas**   - **Interrogativas**

Hoy vamos a aprender cómo preguntar y contestar de una forma positiva.

New: Oraciones positiva

Las oraciones positivas son simples en inglés porque normalmente solo cambia la persona y el verbo queda igual.

- DESEAR   To want

Esto es el infinitivo del verbo, o el verbo sin persona. Así es la forma que el diccionario te va a dar si buscas un verbo nuevo.
En inglés no se cambia el verbo, sino el sujeto o la persona de quién se está hablando:

- WANT – Esto es el base

1. Para decir "yo deseo", ponga I en frente: I want
2. Para decir "tú deseas", ponga YOU en frente: YOU want

La mayoría de la gente usa cuadros verbales para organizar los cambios:

DESEAR/QUERER - TO WANT	
Subject	Conjugation
I	
You	Want

Por ahora solo vamos a aprender la forma I y YOU, pero puedes ver que hay más que aprender en el futuro:

Let's practice!   **Rellena los espacios de los siguientes cuadros verbales:**

Ordenar				Tomar			
Yo	Ordeno			Yo	Tomo		
Tú	Ordenas			Tú	Tomas		
Reservar				Bailar			
Yo	Reservo			Yo	Bailo		
Tú	Reservas			Tú	Bailas		
Cocinar				Esquiar			
Yo	Cocino			Yo	Esquío		
Tú	Cocinas			Tú	Esquías		
Viajar				Desear			
Yo	Viajo			Yo	Deseo		
Tú	Viajas			Tú	Deseas		

Comer				Leer			
Yo	Como			Yo	Leo		
Tú	Comes			Tú	Lees		
Beber				Correr			
Yo	Bebo			Yo	Corro		
Tú	Bebes			Tú	Corres		

Let's practice! Rellena los espacios en blanco con la forma correcta del verbo:

1. _____ _____ (Ordeno) a hotdog.
2. _____ _____ (Tomas) a beer.
3. _____ _____ (Reservo) a table for two.
4. _____ _____ (Deseas) dessert.
5. _____ _____ (Bailas) well.
6. _____ _____ (Cocino) American food.
7. _____ _____ (Esquío) a little.
8. _____ _____ (Viajas) a lot.

New: Making questions (Hacer preguntas)

Vimos antes que la clave de conversar en inglés es poder armar preguntas y contestarlas. La forma interrogativa es muy similar a la forma de TÚ, pero tenemos que empezar la pregunta con **DO**:

Ejemplo:

- Oración con la forma TÚ: You eat hamburgers.
- Pregunta: **Do** you eat hamburgers?

Let's practice! Cambia las siguientes oraciones a preguntas:

1. You eat hamburgers. _____
2. You drink beer. _____
3. You read books. _____
4. You run in the park. _____
5. You read magazines. _____
6. You drink juice. _____
7. You eat hotdogs. _____
8. You run every day. _____

New: Cómo ordenar comida – Ordering food

Hay varias partes de comer en un restaurant - ¡vamos a aprender un diálogo y vocabulario relacionado!

People
Anfitriona – Hostess
Comensal – Guest
Camarera - Server

Menu

Drinks
Soda
Beer
Wine
Water
Orange Juice

Appetizers
French Fries
Chicken wings
Cheese sticks
Salad
Soup

Main Course
Fried Chicken
Hamburger
Grilled steak
Shrimp
Baked Fish

Dessert
Ice Cream
Pie
Cake

Parte 1 – Pedir una mesa
Hostess: How can I help you?
Customer: A table for two, please.

Parte 2 – Ordenar bebidas
Server: Do you want something to drink?
Customer: I want a beer, please.

Parte 3 – Ordenar entradas
Server: Do you want an appetizer?
Customer: I want some onion rings.

Parte 4 – Ordenar el plato fuerte
Server: What do you want to eat today?
Customer: I want the grilled steak.

Parte 5 – Ordenar el postre
Server: Do you want dessert?
Customer: I want some ice cream.

Parte 6 – Pedir la cuenta
Server: Is that all?
Customer: Yes, that is all. Check, please!

Let's practice!   Rellena los espacios en blanco:

Hostess: How can I help you?

Customer: Table for _____, _____ .

Server: Do you want something to drink?

Customer: I want _____ .

Server: Do you want an appetizer?

Customer: I want _____ .

Server: What do you want to eat today?

Customer: I want _____ .

Server: Do you want dessert?

Customer: _____ .

Server: Is that all?

Customer: Yes, _____ . ¡The _____ !

Conversation: American Restaurants

1. Do you eat American food a lot?

    _____

2. What do you order in American restaurants?

    _____

3. Do you drink beer with your food sometimes?

    _____

4. What do you drink normally?

    _____

5. Do you prefer beer or wine with your food?

    _____

6. Do you reserve a table before?

    _____

7. Do you want to eat American food today?

    _____

8. Do you like apple pie?

    _____

Reading: The United States of America

The United States of America is the country to the north of Mexico. According to Wikipedia, there are over 300 million people in the United States. The English from the USA is a different dialect than that of England and there are many different accents.

The capital of the USA is called Washington. It is also known as the District of Columbia or simply DC. It is one of the most beautiful cities in the United States. It is a relatively small city with a population of only 600,000 habitants. The architecture varies greatly and has French, British, and modern influences.

There is no typical American city and there are many interesting places to visit. New York City is known for its variety of cultures and giant skyscrapers. Miami has beautiful beaches and New Orleans has great music and delicious food. Towards the center of the country you can find Denver and the Rocky Mountains and on the west coast Los Angeles is the home of Hollywood and the entertainment industry.

True or false?

1. The United States is south of México.   _____

2. There are many different accents in the USA.   _____

3. Washington is a very big city.   _____

4. The architecture in Washington is not interesting.   _____

5. New York is not an important city.   _____

6. New Orleans is famous for its music and food.   _____

Crédito extra – ¡Visita un restaurante americano y practica ordenar comida en inglés!

And you?

Charmed (to meet you)

To cook

To play soccer

To ski

To travel

To go shopping

To read

To run

To dance

Encantado, Encantada   ¿Y tú?

Jugar fútbol   Cocinar

Viajar   Esquiar

Leer   Ir de compras

Bailar   Correr

Lesson 5

Lesson Highlights

Review
- Shopping
- How to order food

New
- The alphabet
- Pizza
- Conversation

Nuevo: El alfabeto inglés/The English Alphabet

Este cuadro puede ayudarle con la pronunción del alfabeto inglés:

A	E	I	O	U	?
A - E H – Eich J - Ye K – Ke	B – Bi C – Ci D – Di E – I G – Yi P – Pi T – Ti V – Vi Z - Zi	I - Ay Y - Way	O	Q – Kiu U – Iu W – Dabeliu	F – Ef L – El M – Em N – En R – Ar S – Es X - Ecs

A   B   C   D   E   F
(e) (bi) (ci) (di) (i) (ef)

G   H   I   J   K   L
(yi) (eich) (ay) (ye) (ke) (el)

M   N   O   P   Q   R
(em) (en) (o) (pi) (kiu) (ar)

S   T   U   V   W
(es) (ti) (iu) (vi) (dabeliu)

X   Y   Z
(ecs) (huay) (zi)

Puede ver un video aquí:

http://www.youtube.com/watch?v=Fyew85n3XOM

Este es el alfabeto y su pronunciación en los Estados Unidos. Si está en otro país angloparlante, por ejemplo, Inglaterra, es posible que pueda oír un cambio con varias letras. Por ejemplo, la Z puede ser "Zed".

Falta de letras

El alfabeto en inglés solo tiene 26 letras. Fíjese que no existe la Ñ.

New: Deletreando en inglés

Pues ¿por qué estamos aprendiendo el alfabeto si solo queremos hablar el inglés? Constantemente va a encontrarse en situaciones en las cuales será necesario preguntar cómo deletrear las palabras cuando las oye.

Es importantísimo que aprenda el alfabeto muy bien en inglés. Una de las cosas más difíciles del inglés es deletrear.

Ahora, imagínese que estés viajando en los Estados Unidos y tiene que registrarse en el aeropuerto. ¿Qué pasaría si hubieras hecho la reserva, pero deletreaste tu nombre mal? Aquí hay unos ejemplos:

- Juan – Huan
- María – Marea
- David – Dabeed
- Miguel – Meegel

Si no se toma el tiempo de aprender el alfabeto, ¡puede encontrarse en una situación muy incómoda!

Let's practice!   (¡Practiquemos!)

Para hacer la siguiente actividad, necesita saber una pregunta muy fácil en inglés:
¿Cómo se deletrea eso?   How do you spell that?

Siga con lo que necesita saber deletrear. Aquí hay unos ejemplos para practicar:

- **What is your name?**   My name is _____.
- **How do you spell that?**   X-X-X-X-X
- **What is your last name (apellido)?**   It is _____.
- **How do you spell your last name?**   X-X-X-X-X
- **What is your e-mail address?**   It is _____.

New: Shopping and chatting

Hello! How are you?		I am fine, thanks. I need a pencil.
Great! Where are you from?		I am from Guadalajara. And you?
I am from Denver. You speak English well.		Thanks! How much is everything?
One dollar.		See you later!

El diálogo original que aprendió para hacer las compras es bueno, pero muy básico y puede ser solo usado por robots. Los estadounidenses son muy amables y también muy curiosos, así que cuando ven a un extranjero entrando a su tienda probablemente van a tener una conversación con esta persona. Típicamente, la gente preguntará de dónde es y hará un cumplido por hablar bien el inglés, ¡cómo puede ver en este ejemplo!

¡Vamos aprender unas frases para comenzar una conversación en inglés para que puedas extender tus conversaciones al ir de compras!

1. Where are you from?

   _____

2. How old are you?
   - I am _____ years old.
3. Do you like baseball?

   _____

4. What is your favorite team?

   _____

5. What do you like to do?

   _____

6. Are you married?

   _____

7. Why do you speak English?

   _____

8. What do you do?

   _____

9. What are you doing here in the United States?

   _____

10. Do you like to listen to _____ music?
    a. Rock and Roll
    b. Jazz
    c. Pop
    d. Hip hop/Rap

Lets practice! Cree un nuevo diálogo e incluya unas de estas frases para tener una conversación:

Clerk: _____

Customer: _____

Clerk: _____

Customer: _____

Clerk: _____

Customer: _____

Clerk: _____

Customer: _____

Clerk: _____

Customer: _____

Clerk: _____

Customer: _____

Clerk: _____

Customer: _____

Review - Colors

GROUP A	GROUP B	GROUP C	GROUP D	GROUP E	GROUP F	GROUP G	GROUP H
RUSSIA	PORTUGAL	FRANCE	ARGENTINA	BRAZIL	GERMANY	BELGIUM	POLAND
SAUDI ARABIA	SPAIN	AUSTRALIA	ICELAND	SWITZERLAND	MEXICO	PANAMA	SENEGAL
EGYPT	MOROCCO	PERU	CROATIA	COSTA RICA	SWEDEN	TUNISIA	COLOMBIA
URUGUAY	IR IRAN	DENMARK	NIGERIA	SERBIA	KOREA REP.	ENGLAND	JAPAN

1. What are the colors of the German team? _____
2. What are the colors of the Argentine team? _____
3. What are the colors of the Brazilian team? _____
4. What are the colors of the Australian team? _____
5. What are the colors of the Belgian team? _____
6. What are the colors of the French team? _____
7. What are the colors of the Swiss team? _____
8. What are the colors of the Nigerian team? _____

New – Famous Americans

Barack Obama was the president of the United States. He is the first African American president and is very popular around the world. Unfortunately, because of the Great Recession of 2008 and gun violence, his presidency was controversial. He is either loved or hated by the American public.

John F Kennedy was the US President that tried to invade Cuba in 1961 to fight communism in Latin America but failed. He was assassinated in 1963.

Jay-Z is a rapper and entrepreneur from New York and considered to be one of the best of all time. He is married to Beyoncé, an R&B singer, and together they are considered one of the most powerful and richest couples in the world.

Marc Anthony and Jennifer Lopez are famous singers, but are known for having one of the most jealous and ugly public relationships.

George Lopez is a Chicano comedian from Los Angeles and uses a lot of "Spanglish" in his comedy.

Cheech and Chong is a comedic duo that is active since the 70's. They are very popular among people that smoke marijuana.

Bill Gates is the most well known businessman from the US and is sometimes known as the richest man in the world.

Al Sharpton is a famous Baptist minister and a civil rights leader that fights for justice and equality, especially for black Americans.

1. Do you like Barack Obama? _____
2. Do you like John F Kennedy? _____
3. Do you like Jay-Z and Beyoncé? _____
4. Do you like Marc Anthony y Jennifer Lopez? _____
5. Do you like George Lopez? _____
6. Do you like Cheech and Chong? _____
7. Do you like Bill Gates? _____
8. Do you like Al Sharpton? _____

Review – Regular verbs:

Ordenar				Tomar			
Yo	Ordeno			Yo	Tomo		
Tú	Ordenas			Tú	Tomas		
Reservar				Bailar			
Yo	Reservo			Yo	Bailo		
Tú	Reservas			Tú	Bailas		
Cocinar				Esquiar			
Yo	Cocino			Yo	Esquió		
Tú	Cocinas			Tú	Esquías		
Viajar				Desear			
Yo	Viajo			Yo	Deseo		
Tú	Viajas			Tú	Deseas		

Comer				Leer			
Yo	Como			Yo	Leo		
Tú	Comes			Tú	Lees		
Beber				Correr			
Yo	Bebo			Yo	Corro		
Tú	Bebes			Tú	Corres		

1. Do you order orange juice with breakfast?

2. Do you drink coffee in the morning?

3. Do you normally reserve a table?

4. Do you dance at the club?

5. Do you cook American food?

6. Do you ski a lot during the winter?

7. Do you travel around the US?

8. What do you want to drink today?

9. Do you order Italian food often?

10. How many glasses of water do you drink generally?

11. Do you read a lot?

12. Do you run outside or at the gym?

New: Making Questions

Para tener un nivel conversacional en inglés, tiene que poder cambiar de preguntar en la forma interrogativa de "YOU" y poder contestar en la forma de "I".

Vamos a practicar hacer preguntas:

Example:

Do you drink beer?
Yes, I drink beer.

> Verbs
> Drink | Order | Want

Tema - Bebidas (drinks)

1. **Orange juice**
a. Pregunta: _____
b. Respuesta: _____

2. **Apple juice**
a. Pregunta: _____
b. Respuesta: _____

3. **Coffee**
a. Pregunta: _____
b. Respuesta: _____

4. **Milk**
a. Pregunta: _____
b. Respuesta: _____

5. **Water**
a. Pregunta: _____
b. Respuesta: _____

6. **Soda**
a. Pregunta: _____
b. Respuesta: _____

7. **Beer**
a. Pregunta: _____
b. Respuesta: _____

8. **Wine**
a. Pregunta: _____
b. Respuesta: _____

9. **Cocktails**
a. Pregunta: _____

b. Respuesta: _____

10. **Rum**
a. Pregunta: _____
b. Respuesta: _____

Tema – Comidas (meals)

> Verbs
> Eat | Cook | Order | Want

1. **Breakfast**
a. Question: _____
b. Answer: _____

2. **Lunch**
a. Question: _____
b. Answer: _____

3. **Dinner**
a. Question: _____
b. Answer: _____

4. **Eggs**
a. Question: _____
b. Answer: _____
5. **Rice**
a. Question: _____
b. Answer: _____

6. **Beef**
a. Question: _____
b. Answer: _____

7. **Fruit**
a. Question: _____
b. Answer: _____

8. **Vegetables**
a. Question: _____
b. Answer: _____

9. **Chicken**
a. Question: _____
b. Answer: _____

10. **Fish**

a. Question: _____

b. Answer: _____

Review: How to order food

Use la carta en la próxima pagina para ordenar comida.

Hostess: How can I help you?

Customer: Table for _____.

Server: What do you want to drink?

Customer: I want _____.

Server: Do you want an appetizer?

Customer: I want _____.

Server: What do you want to eat today?

Customer: I want _____.

Server: Do you want dessert?

Customer: _____.

Server: Is that all?

Customer : Yes, _____. The

_____!

Anthony's Pizza & Pasta

Drinks
Soda $1.79
Beer...............$4.99
Glass of Wine...$5.99
Bottle of Water...$1.75
Lemonade.........$1.99

Appetizers
Garlic bread..............$3.99
Buffalo Wings..........$6.55
Cheese sticks........$6.65
Caesar Salad............$2.99

Sandwiches and Pasta
Meatball.......$6.99
Italian Sausage..$7.99
Spaghetti...$9.99
Cheese Ravioli.....$8.99

New York Style Pizza
Cheese......$2.75
Pepperoni.........$3.24
Hawaiian...$3.73
Veggie....$3.99

Dessert
Ice Cream $1.99
(Vanilla,Strawberry, Chocolate, Dulce de leche)
Cheesecake...$4.99
Brownie..............$5.99

New: Culture – New York

New York is located in the northeastern part of the United States and is the largest city by population with more than 8 million residents. It has the largest Jewish population in the Americas.

New York is a true "melting pot" of cultures and about half of the people speak a language other than English. It is well known for its Italian American residents. Many people believe that New York style pizza is the best in the world.

The architecture is amazing and consists of some of the tallest skyscrapers in the world, like the Empire State Building. New York has all types of sports teams, including 4 soccer teams, 2 football teams, 2 hockey teams, 2 basketball teams, and 2 baseball teams. New Yorkers argue that it is the greatest city in the world.

True or false?
1. New York City is a small city. _____
2. More than 8 million people live in New York. _____
3. The Jewish religion is not important in New York. _____
4. Sports are very popular in New York. _____
5. New York doesn't have good pizza. _____
6. There is nothing interesting to see in New York. _____

New: Vocabulary – Actividades cotidianas (Daily activities)

1. Hablar/Talk
2. Caminar/Walk
3. Correr/Run
4. Aprender/Learn
5. Escribir/Write
6. Recibir/Receive, Get
7. Vivir/Live
8. Discutir/Argue

Talk   Walk

Run   Learn

Write   Receive
                        Get

Live   Argue

How old are you?   I am thirty years old.

Caminar

Hablar

Aprender

Correr

Recibir

Escribir

Discutir

Vivir

Tengo treinta años.

¿Cuántos años tienes?

Lesson 6

Lesson Highlights

Review
- Verbs – Questions and answers
- The alphabet

New
- Negative
- Prepositions and phrases
- Days of the week
- Months of the year

Review: How much does it cost?

1. How much is a glass of wine? ($6) _____
2. How much is a soda? ($1) _____
3. How much is an orange juice? ($3) _____
4. How much is a beer? ($5) _____
5. How much is a steak? ($10) _____
6. How much is a sandwich?($7) _____
7. How much is a pizza? ($8) _____
8. How much is an ice cream?($2) _____

Repaso: El alfabeto

¿Recuerdas cómo decir el alfabeto en inglés? Inténtelo:

A B C D E F
G H I J K L
M N O P Q
R S T U V
W X Y Z

Repaso: ¿Cómo se deletrea?

- **What is your name?** My name is _____.
- **How do you spell that?** X-X-X-X-X
- **What is your last name (apellido)?** It is _____.
- **How do you spell your last name?** X-X-X-X-X
- **What is your e-mail address?** It is _____.

New – Actividades Cotidianas/Everyday activities

Vamos a repasar nuestros verbos y cómo se conjugan para hablar de las actividades cotidianas.

Verbs

Hablar				Caminar			
Yo	hablo			Yo	camino		
Tu	hablas			Tu	caminas		
Correr				Aprender			
Yo	corro			Yo	aprendo		
Tu	corres			Tu	aprendes		

New: Negative

Hay una forma más que aprender – la forma negativa.

Ejemplo: VIVIR – To live

Recuerda que en inglés no se cambia el verbo, sino el sujeto o la persona de quien está hablando:

- Para decir yo vivo, ponga I en frente: I live
- Para decir no vivo, ponga DO NOT entre I y LIVE: I do not live
- Para decir tú vives, ponga YOU en frente: You live
- Para decir tú no vives, ponga DO NOT entre YOU y LIVE: You do not live

Let's practice! Rellena las cajas del siguiente cuadro:

Escribir				Recibir			
Yo	No escribo			Yo	No recibo		
Tú	No escribes			Tú	No recibes		
Conversar				Vivir			
Yo	No discuto			Yo	No vivo		
Tú	No discutes			Tú	No vives		

Be careful! **Cognados falsos** – Antes aprendimos que los cognados son palabras en inglés que son fáciles de adivinar porque comparten una misma raíz latina con la palabra en español.

Desafortunadamente tenemos también los cognados falsos, que son palabras compartidas en la raíz latina, pero por alguna razón la traducción es diferente.

Discuss es un ejemplo de un cognado falso. Se supone que significa discutir, pero en realidad tiene un significado positivo — conversar. Discutir quiere decir *argue* en inglés. Imagina decirle a su maestro que quiere conversar de algo después de clase. ¿Se sentiría incómodo decirle "discuss", no? Sin embargo, en inglés es normal y suena bien.

Let's practice!

1. _____ (No hablo) with my mom.
2. _____ (No caminas) in the park.
3. _____ (No corro) in the gym.

4. _____ (No aprendes) English
5. _____ (No vives) in Denver.
6. _____ (No escribo) an e-mail to my friend.
7. _____ (No recibes) a lot of junk mail.
8. _____ (No converso) with my husband/wife.

New - Conversation

1. Do you talk a lot with your mom?

   _____

2. Do you walk/hike in the mountains?

   _____

3. Do you run in the park every day?

   _____

4. Do you learn English right now?

   _____

5. Do you live in a house or an apartment?

   _____

6. Do you write e-mails every day?

   _____

7. Do you receive too much junk mail?

   _____

8. Do you argue with your colleagues a lot?

   _____

New - Prepositions and phrases

Por es una preposición en español, y desafortunadamente las preposiciones son palabras difíciles de traducir y pueden significar varias cosas en inglés.
- Medio de comunicación – On the phone, via email, in the mail, etc.
- Movimiento general, ubicación – Around/through/by
- Horario aproximado – Around/about/ish

1. _____ (no hablas) on the pone on Sundays.

2. _____ (no camino) through / in the mountains on the weekend.

3. _____ (no corres) around the park on Saturdays.

4. _____ (no aprendes) English in the morning.

5. _____ (no escribo) via email.

6. _____ (no vivo) in the North of Denver.

7. _____ (no discutes) on the phone.

8. _____ (no recibo) a letter in the mail.

Review – Making questions

Usa las frases de abajo con los verbos de arriba para formar preguntas en la forma de **you** y contéstalas en la forma de I:

> Talk | Walk | Order | Drink | Reserve | Want | Dance | Travel

1. **On the phone**
   a. Pregunta: _____
   b. Respuesta: _____
2. **Around the park**
   a. Pregunta: _____
   b. Respuesta: _____
3. **Through the mountains**
   a. Pregunta: _____
   b. Respuesta: _____
4. **Beer**
   a. Pregunta: _____
   b. Respuesta: _____
5. **Rum**
   a. Pregunta: _____
   b. Respuesta: _____
6. **A table for your family**
   a. Pregunta: _____
   b. Respuesta: _____
7. **Appetizers**
   a. Pregunta: _____
   b. Respuesta: _____
8. **Dessert**
   a. Pregunta: _____
   b. Respuesta: _____
9. **A lot**
   a. Pregunta: _____
   b. Respuesta: _____
10. **Little**
   a. Pregunta: _____
   b. Respuesta: _____

| Drink | Eat | Run | Learn |

1. **Wine**

    a. Pregunta: _____

    b. Respuesta: _____

2. **English**

    a. Pregunta: _____

    b. Respuesta: _____

3. **At the gym**

    a. Pregunta: _____

    b. Respuesta: _____

4. **Something interesting**

    a. Pregunta: _____

    b. Respuesta: _____

5. **8 glasses of water**

    a. Pregunta: _____

    b. Respuesta: _____

6. **Italian**

    a. Pregunta: _____

    b. Respuesta: _____

7. **In the morning**

    a. Pregunta: _____

    b. Respuesta: _____

8. **Beef**

    a. Pregunta: _____

    b. Respuesta: _____

9. **In public**

    a. Pregunta: _____

    b. Respuesta: _____

10. **Sweets**

    a. Pregunta: _____

    b. Respuesta: _____

1. **In Denver**

    a. Pregunta: _____

    b. Respuesta: _____

2. **Poetry**

    a. Pregunta: _____

    b. Respuesta: _____

3. **Email**

    a. Pregunta: _____

    b. Respuesta: _____

4. **Junk mail**

    a. Pregunta: _____

    b. Respuesta: _____

5. **In a house**

    a. Pregunta: _____

    b. Respuesta: _____

6. **About your work**

    a. Pregunta: _____

    b. Respuesta: _____

7. **A love letter**

    a. Pregunta: _____

    b. Respuesta: _____

8. **Close to the school**

    a. Pregunta: _____

    b. Respuesta: _____

9. **A book**

    a. Pregunta: _____

    b. Respuesta: _____

10. **With your love**

    a. Pregunta: _____

    b. Respuesta: _____

New – Days of the week

Lunes/Monday
Martes/Tuesday
Miércoles/Wednesday
Jueves/Thursday

Viernes/Friday
Sábado/Saturday
Domingo/Sunday

1. What day is today? _____

2. Do you like Mondays? _____

3. What is your favorite day of the week? _____

4. What is your least favorite? _____

> • Los días de la semana siempre empiezan con mayúsculas en inglés.
> • En inglés se usa la palabra "ON" para hablar de un evento venidero.
> • Para hablar de eventos habituales se usa la forma plural del día, pero no se usa el artículo

5. Do you drink coffee on Mondays? _____

6. Do you work on Tuesdays? _____

7. Do you study English on Wednesdays? _____

8. Do you ski on Thursdays? _____

9. Do you drink beer on Fridays? _____

10. Do you dance on Saturdays? _____

11. Do you rest on Sundays? _____

New – Numbers 11-31

11 eleven	18 eighteen	25 twenty-five
12 twelve	19 nineteen	26 twenty-six
13 thirteen	20 twenty	27 twenty-seven
14 fourteen	21 twenty-one	28 twenty-eight
15 fifteen	22 twenty-two	29 twenty-nine
16 sixteen	23 twenty-three	30 thirty
17 seventeen	24 twenty-four	31 thirty-one

New – Months of the year

1. **Enero/January**
2. **Febrero/February**
3. **Marzo/March**
4. **Abril/April**
5. **Mayo/May**
6. **Junio/June**
7. **Julio/July**
8. **Agosto/August**
9. **Septiembre/September**
10. **Octubre/October**
11. **Noviembre/November**
12. **Diciembre/December**

New – La fecha/The date

En inglés se dice primero el mes y después el día.
- Example: Today is November 22nd.

También en inglés se usa el número ordinal (First, second, third, fourth, etc.).
- Today is November 1st.

1. What is today's date? _____
2. What is yesterday's date? _____
3. What is tomorrow's date? _____
4. When is your birthday? _____
5. What is your favorite holiday? _____
6. What is the date of your anniversary? _____

Nuevo: Escuchar/Listening

Escucha esta canción en YouTube con el enlace abajo y sigue la letra, o "lyrics":
https://www.youtube.com/watch?v=wa2nLEhUcZ0

The Cure – Friday I'm In Love

No me importa si el lunes es azul	I don't care if Monday's blue
Si el martes es gris y el miércoles también	Tuesday's grey and Wednesday too
El jueves no me importas	Thursday I don't care about you
Es viernes, estoy enamorado	It's Friday I'm in love
En lunes puedes desbaratarte	Monday you can fall apart
El martes, miércoles me rompen el corazón	Tuesday, Wednesday break my heart
El jueves ni siquiera empieza	Thursday doesn't even start
Es viernes, estoy enamorado	It's Friday I'm in love
El sábado, espera	Saturday wait
Y el domingo siempre viene demasiado tarde	and Sunday always comes too late
Pero el viernes nunca vacila	But Friday never hesitate...
No me importa si el lunes es negro	I don't care if Monday's black
Martes, miércoles un infarto	Tuesday, Wednesday heart attack
Jueves nunca mirando para atrás	Thursday never looking back
Es viernes, estoy enamorado	It's Friday I'm in love
Lunes te puedes aguantar la cabeza	Monday you can hold your head
Martes, miércoles quédate en la cama	Tuesday, Wednesday stay in bed
O jueves ver las paredes en lugar de eso	Or Thursday watch the walls instead
Es viernes, estoy enamorado	It's Friday I'm in love
Sábado, espera	Saturday wait
Y domingo siempre viene demasiado tarde	and Sunday always comes too late
Pero viernes nunca vacila	But Friday never hesitate...
Vestido hasta los ojos, es una sorpresa maravillosa el ver tus zapatos y tus espíritus subirse	Dressed up to the eyes It's a wonderful surprise to see your shoes and your spirits rise
Quitándose la cara triste y simplemente sonriendo con el sonido y tan liso como un grito dándose vueltas Siempre muerde una mordida grande	Throwing out your frown And just smiling at the sound And as sleek as a shriek Spinning round and round
Es tan bello el vistazo de verte comer por la media noche	Always take a big bite
Tú nunca puedes conseguir suficiente de estas cosas	It's such a gorgeous sight To see you eat in the middle of the night
Es viernes, estoy enamorado	You can never get enough, enough of this stuff It's Friday I'm in love
No me importa si el lunes es azul	I don't care if Monday's blue
Martes gris y miércoles también	Tuesday's grey and Wednesday too
Jueves no me importas	Thursday I don't care about you
Es viernes, estoy enamorado	It's Friday, I'm in love
Lunes, puedes desbaratarte	Monday you can fall apart
Martes, miércoles me rompen el corazón	Tuesday, Wednesday break my heart Thursday doesn't even start
Jueves ni siquiera empieza	It's Friday I'm in love
Es viernes, estoy enamorado	

New: American Culture and Cities

DAD es un sufijo común en español que típicamente traduce a *TY* en inglés:

Ciu**dad** – City   Universi**dad** – Universi**ty**
Reali**dad** – Reali**ty**   posibili**dad** – Possibili**ty**

Las palabras que terminan con -*ty* casi siempre son cognados y pueden ser adivinadas.

Denver is the capital of the state of Colorado and currently it is growing faster than any other city in the United States. As with most American cities, downtown there is a large urban area filled with skyscrapers and government buildings surrounded by residential neighborhoods and suburbs where most families live. Sports are very popular and Denver is home to a baseball team, a basketball team, a hockey team, a soccer team, and the residents are very proud of their championship football team, the Denver Broncos. There is a good music scene and Red Rocks is a beautiful place to see a concert. Major artists from all over the world come to play shows frequently. Denver and the state of Colorado are famous for outdoor activities like skiing and mountain biking too. In most recent years Denver leads a new industry and is now famous for legal marijuana.

English Names

In English speaking countries most people have 3 names, including their first name, middle name, and last name.

Ex: George Timothy Clooney

There is only one last name because English speakers usually use the family name of the father.

Depending on the person, most people use their first name and rarely mention their middle name.

True or False?

1. Denver is the capital of the United States and the largest city. _____
2. There are no skyscrapers in Denver. _____
3. Marijuana is legal in Colorado. _____
4. It is rare to see people outside in Colorado. _____
5. The Denver Broncos is an excellent football team. _____
6. People in the US normally have 4 names. _____

Monday	Tuesday
Wednesday	Thursday
Friday	Saturday
Sunday	January
February	March

Martes	Lunes
Jueves	Miércoles
Sábado	Viernes
Enero	Domingo
Marzo	Febrero

April

May

June

July

August

September

October

November

December

It's June 13th.

Mayo   Abril

Julio   Junio

Septiembre   Agosto

Noviembre   Octubre

Es el 13 de junio.   Diciembre

Lesson 7

Lesson Highlights

Review
- Making questions
- Dates
- Daily activities

New
- Time
- Numbers 0-100

- Su – His/Her
- 3rd person - Gossip
- Reading activity – Team sports in the US
- Bargaining
- Conjunciones
- Family

Review: Making questions

> Talk | Walk | Order | Drink | Reserve | Want | Dance | Travel

1. **Online**

    a. Question: _____

    b. Answer: _____

2. **Appetizers**

    a. Question: _____

    b. Answer: _____

3. **A lot of water**

    a. Question: _____

    b. Answer: _____

4. **Alcohol**

    a. Question: _____

    b. Answer: _____

5. **Sodas**

    a. Question: _____

    b. Answer: _____

6. **A table**

    a. Question: _____

    b. Answer: _____

7. **A hotel**

a. Question: _____

b. Answer: _____

8. **Movie tickets**

   a. Question: _____

   b. Answer: _____

9. **Hip hop**

   a. Question: _____

   b. Answer: _____

10. **Ballet**

    a. Question: _____

    b. Answer: _____

Drink | Eat | Run | Learn

1. **Beef**

   a. Question: _____

   b. Answer: _____

2. **Sweets**

   a. Question: _____

   b. Answer: _____

3. **Out a lot**

   a. Question: _____

   b. Answer: _____

4. **Milk**

   a. Question: _____

   b. Answer: _____

5. **Cocktails**

   a. Question: _____

   b. Answer: _____

6. **Orange juice**

   a. Question: _____

   b. Answer: _____

7. **At the gym**

    a. Question: _____

    b. Answer: _____

8. **With your dog**

    a. Question: _____

    b. Answer: _____

9. **Everyday**

    a. Question: _____

    b. Answer: _____

10. **English**

    a. Question: _____

    b. Answer: _____

11. **Something interesting**

    a. Question: _____

    b. Answer: _____

12. **History**

    a. Question: _____

    b. Answer: _____

> Live | Write | Get | Argue

1. **With someone**

    a. Question: _____

    b. Answer: _____

2. **In Denver**

    a. Question: _____

    b. Answer: _____

3. **Close to here**

    a. Question: _____

    b. Answer: _____

4. **Poetry**

    a. Question: _____

b. Answer: _____

5. **Love letters**

   a. Question: _____

   b. Answer: _____

6. **Email**

   a. Question: _____

   b. Answer: _____

7. **Invitations to parties**

   a. Question: _____

   b. Answer: _____

8. **Political mail**

   a. Question: _____

   b. Answer: _____

9. **Friends at your house**

   a. Question: _____

   b. Answer: _____

10. **With your friends**

   a. Question: _____

   b. Answer: _____

11. **About politics**

   a. Question: _____

   b. Answer: _____

12. **Often**

   a. Question: _____

   b. Answer: _____

Review: The date

How do you say_____?

1. 1° de enero	_____	6. 13 de junio	_____
2. 2 de febrero	_____	7. 4 de julio	_____
3. 17 de marzo	_____	8. 16 de agosto	_____
4. 1° de abril	_____	9. 11 de septiembre	_____
5. 5 de mayo	_____	10. 30 de octubre	_____

11. 27 de noviembre _____   12. 25 de diciembre _____

What is today's date?   _____

New: Numbers 0 - 100

El primero paso para aprender contar hasta 100 es aprender los números de base:

0 – Zero	40 – Forty	80 – Eighty
10 – Ten	50 – Fifty	90 – Ninety
20 – Twenty	60 – Sixty	100 – One hundred
30 – Thirty	70 – Seventy	

Después de 20, simplemente agrega un guion más el número:

20 twenty	24 twenty-four	28 twenty-eight
21 twenty-one	25 twenty-five	29 twenty-nine
22 twenty-two	26 twenty-six	
23 twenty-three	27 twenty-seven	

Puede seguir este modelo hasta el cien:

21 – Twenty-one	54 – Fifty-four	87 – Eighty-seven
32 – Thirty-two	65 – Sixty-five	98 – Ninety-eight
43 – Forty-three	76 – Seventy-six	100 – One hundred

Let's practice!

Siempre es buena idea preguntar por el precio antes de comprar algo. ¡Es una buena manera practicar con los números también!

How much does _____ cost?

Breakfast   _____

Lunch   _____

Dinner   _____

How much do _____ cost?

Appetizers

Cuando pregunta por el precio de cosas (plural), does cambia a do.

Entrées   _____

Desserts   _____

Ahora imagínate que te fuiste de vacaciones y te olvidaste traer unas cosas. Aquí tenemos una lista de necesidades para viajar por el caso de tener que reemplazar algo:

Toiletries/ Artículos de aseo	Clothes/Ropa	Souvenirs/Recuerdos
Toothbrush/Cepillo dental	Socks/Calcetines	Hat/Gorra

Toothpaste/Crema dental	Underwear/Ropa interior	T-shirt/Camiseta
Deodorant/Desodorante	Belt/Cinturón	Poster/Afiche
Comb/Peine	Pants/Pantalones	Towel/Toalla

How much do/does the _____ cost?

1. Toothpaste _____
2. Combs _____
3. Toothbrushes _____
4. Deodorant _____
5. Pants _____
6. Underwear _____
7. Belts _____
8. Socks _____
9. Hat _____
10. Towels _____
11. Shirt _____
12. Poster _____

New - Bargaining

Bargaining, o regatear, is not common in the United States, especially in normal stores and most gift shops. It is more common for expensive purchases like cars and houses. If you don't like a price, simply do not buy it.

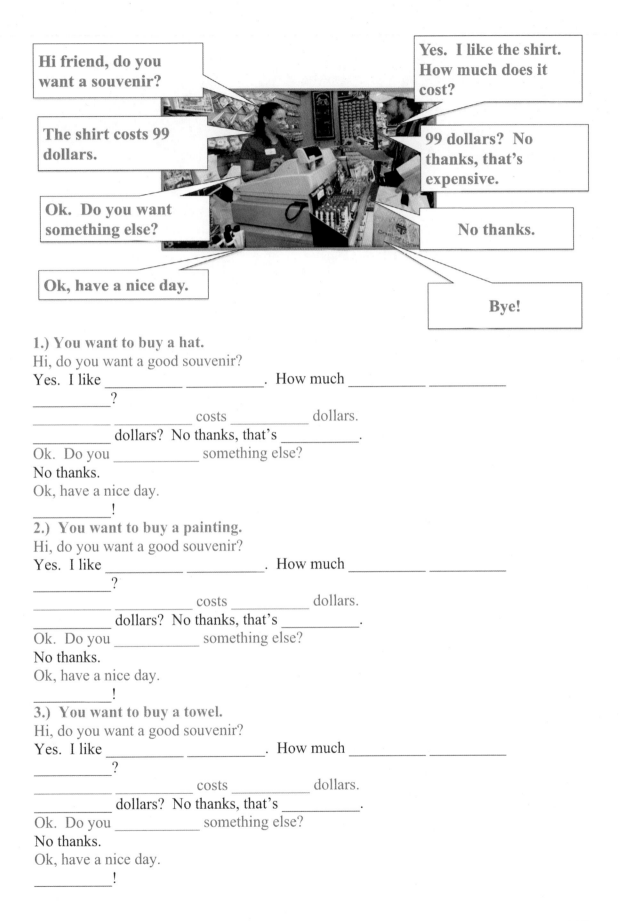

Hi friend, do you want a souvenir?

Yes. I like the shirt. How much does it cost?

The shirt costs 99 dollars.

99 dollars? No thanks, that's expensive.

Ok. Do you want something else?

No thanks.

Ok, have a nice day.

Bye!

1.) You want to buy a hat.
Hi, do you want a good souvenir?
Yes. I like _____ _____. How much _____ _____
_____?
_____ _____ costs _____ dollars.
_____ dollars? No thanks, that's _____.
Ok. Do you _____ something else?
No thanks.
Ok, have a nice day.
_____!

2.) You want to buy a painting.
Hi, do you want a good souvenir?
Yes. I like _____ _____. How much _____ _____
_____?
_____ _____ costs _____ dollars.
_____ dollars? No thanks, that's _____.
Ok. Do you _____ something else?
No thanks.
Ok, have a nice day.
_____!

3.) You want to buy a towel.
Hi, do you want a good souvenir?
Yes. I like _____ _____. How much _____ _____
_____?
_____ _____ costs _____ dollars.
_____ dollars? No thanks, that's _____.
Ok. Do you _____ something else?
No thanks.
Ok, have a nice day.
_____!

4.) You want to buy a shirt.

Hi, do you want a good souvenir?

Yes. I like _____ _____. How much _____ _____ _____?

_____ _____ costs _____ dollars.

_____ dollars? No thanks, that's _____.

Ok. Do you _____ something else?

No thanks.

Ok, have a nice day.

_____!

Nuevo – Las conjunciones And/Or

Conjunciones son palabras que crean conexiónes entre palabras y frases.
- And - Y
- Or - O

son las más comunes.

Question: Do you want water or beer?
Answer: I want water and beer!

Let's practice!

1. Do you want more money, or more free time?

    _____

2. Do you talk more with your family or your friends?

    _____

3. Do you often walk in the park or trhe mountains?

    _____

4. Do you order appetizers or dessert at the restaurant?

    _____

5. Do you drink wine or beer?

    _____

6. Do you dance to salsa or bachata?

    _____

7. Do you travel more to the mountains or the beach?

    _____

8. Do you drink coffee or tea in the morning?

    _____

9. Do you eat American food or Mexican food more?

    _____

10. Do you normally run inside or outside?

    _____

11. Do you live in the city or the suburbs?

_____

12. Do you write text messages or make phone calls?

_____

New: Time

Solo hay una manera decir la hora en inglés:

What time is it?

1:00 – It is one o'clock.
2:00 – It is two o'clock.

- Siempre se dice "it is" más la hora
- No importa si es singular o plural

What time is it?

7:23 – It is seven twenty-three.

- Para agregar los minutos, dilos normalmente sin nada más.
- Cuando se trata de minutos menos de diez, puedes decir "oh" antes de los minutos.

Let's practice!

What time is it?

| 12:08 | 6:38 | 4:00 |

_____ _____ _____

| 10:10 | 3:45 | 8:24 |

_____ _____ _____

1. What time is it now?   _____
2. What is today's date?   _____
3. When is your birthday?   _____
4. At what time do you wake up? _____
5. At what time do your work?   _____

121

6. At what time to you get home? _____
7. At what time do you go to sleep? _____

New – 3ʳᵈ person – Gossip

Vamos a seguir mejorando nuestras capacidades conversacionales y aprender a hablar en la tercera persona. ¡En otras palabras, vamos a aprender a chismear!

Para ayudarte con estos conceptos gramaticales, los verbos son conjugados por persona, 1ª, 2ª, 3ª. Hasta ahora, hemos aprendido las formas de 1ª y 2ª en inglés:

1ª persona - Yo vivo en Denver. I live in Denver.
Se llama la primera persona porque estoy hablando de mí mismo y nadie más necesita estar involucrado en la conversación.

2ª persona - Tú vives en Denver. You live in Denver.
Se llama la segunda persona porque estoy hablando contigo y necesitamos dos personas involucradas en esta conversación.

3ª persona - David vive en Denver. David lives in Denver.
Se llama la tercera persona porque estoy hablando contigo sobre David, y ahora tenemos tres personas involucradas en la conversación.

Verbos S

Example: Want

El único cambio verbal de los verbos regulares en inglés viene en la tercera persona.

Para decir que él/ella desea, agrega S   He/She wants

DESEAR – TO WANT/DESIRE		
Persona		Singular
1ª	I	Want
2ª	You	Want
3ª	He She	Wants

Verbos ES

Hay que agregar ES a los verbos que terminan con O o los que producen el sonido de S (S, SH, CH, X, ZZ)

Example: Do

Para decir que él/ella hace, agrega ES   He/She does

HACER – TO DO		
Persona		Singular
1ª	I	Do
2ª	You	Do
3ª	He She	Does

Verbos IES

Verbos que terminan con un consonante seguido por la letra Y tienen otra regla:

- Cambia la
- Agrega ES

ESTUDIAR – TO STUDY		
Person		Singular
1ª	I	Study
2ª	You	Study
3ª	He She	Studies

Y por I

Ex: Study

Para decir que él/ella estudia, cambia la Y por I y agrega ES   He/She studies

Let's practice!

1. He _____ (talk) with his brother.
2. She _____ (walk) every day.
3. David _____ (do) homework.
4. Luis _____ (order) a hamburger.
5. She _____ (study) English.
6. My sister _____ (do) chores.
7. Your cousin _____ (fly) to Washington.
8. Sandra _____ (drink) a cold beer.
9. He _____ (finish) his work for the day.
10. The pope _____ (try) to help a lot of people.

New – 3rd Person Negative

En el negativo, se usa la forma del verbo normal, pero hay que poner DOES NOT primero. El verbo no cambia:

He does not want food right now.

*Fíjese que el verbo "*WANT*" queda en la forma infinitiva porque cambiamos el verbo auxiliar *DO* a *DOES*.

Let's practice!
1. He _____ (talk) with his brother.
2. She _____ (walk) every day.
3. David _____ (do) homework.
4. Luis _____ (order) a hamburger.
5. She _____ (study) English.
6. My sister _____ (do) chores.
7. Your cousin _____ (fly) to Washington.
8. Sandra _____ (drink) a cold beer.
9. He _____ (finish) his work for the day.
10. The pope _____ (try) to help a lot of people.

New – Family
1. Does your grandpa live in Denver?

_____

2. Does your grandma write poetry?

_____

3. Does your mom get email?

_____

4. Does your dad get junk mail?

_____

5. Does your brother live in a house?

_____

6. Does your sister write a love letter?

_____

7. Does someone in your family live close to the school?

_____

8. Does someone in your family write a book?

_____

Now, thinking about your best friend….

13. Does he/she talk on the phone?

_____

14. Does he/she walk around the park?

_____

15. Does he/she hike in the mountains?

_____

16. Does he/she drink beer?

_____

17. Does he/she drink rum?

_____

18. Does he/she reserve a table at a restaurant?

_____

19. Does he/she order appetizers?

_____

20. Does he/she order dessert?

_____

21. Does he/she talk a lot?

_____

22. Does he/she talk little?

_____

Nuevo: His | Her = Su

SU = HIS, HER

Es interesante que la palabra SU es his and her en Inglés.

What is **his** name?
His name is Mike.

What is **her** name?
Her name is Mary.

Let's practice!

- What is her name?
- _____ _____ _____ Sandra.

- What is her name?
- _____ name _____ Madonna.

- What is his name?
- _____ name _____ "The Rock".

- What is his name?
- _____ name _____ Al.

- What is her name?
- _____ _____ _____ Beyoncé.

- What is his name?
- _____ name _____ Will.

- What is his name?
- _____ name _____ Leonardo.

- What is her name?
- _____ _____ _____ Oprah.

1. What is your dad's name?   _____
2. What is your mom's name?   _____
3. What is your spouse's name?   _____
4. What is your dog's name?   _____
5. What is your best friend's name? _____
6. What is your boss's name?   _____
7. What is your teacher's name?   _____
8. What is your favorite singer's name?   _____

New – Reading: Team Sports in the United States

Americans love to watch team sports. Sports are little different in the United States. One of the main differences is the variety of sports that Americans watch. The four most popular sports are Football, Baseball, Basketball, and Hockey. Soccer is not traditionally a very popular, but it is growing in popularity now.

There are 11 players on a Football team. To win, you score points primarily by making a touchdown for six points. After a touchdown, you have the opportunity score an extra point by kicking the ball through the uprights. Teams can also score by kicking field goals for three points, making a two-point conversion after a touchdown, or by tackling the opposing team in its own end zone for a two-point safety. Football is a very complicated game.

Baseball is called the "national pastime" in the United States. It is the oldest team sport in the US. There are 9 players on a Baseball team. One team bats while the other team fields. To score, a player must hit the bal, and then run all four bases to successfully touch home base for a "run" that is worth 1 point. A fan favorite is when a batter hits the ball past the outfield for a homerun. If first base, second base, and third base are all occupied when the batter hits the homerun, it's called a grand slam, and worth four points.

Basketball is considered the third most popular sport in the US. Each team consists of five players. Players dribble the ball down the court and shoot baskets for two or three points, depending on the distance of the shot. A slam dunk occurs when a player jumps up and directly places the ball in the basket.

Ice Hockey is another very popular team sport in the US, although it is originally from Canada. There are six players that ice skate and use a long L-shaped stick to try and hit the puck in the opponent's goal for a point. Although it is officially prohibited, fighting is also a major part of the game. At least one fight normally occurs during each game.

Finally, soccer is the last of the most popular team sports that is played professionally. It is starting to be more popular, but most Americans do not watch it very consistently. It has the same rules here as in other countries.

True or false?

1. Americans don't like to watch sports.   _____
2. A touchdown is worth seven points.   _____
3. Baseball is the national pastime in the US.   _____
4. There are nine players on a baseball team.   _____
5. Basketball is the most popular sport in the US.   _____
6. You can make a slam dunk in basketball.   _____
7. Ice Hockey is not from the United States.   _____
8. Fighting is allowed in Ice Hockey.   _____
9. Soccer is the most popular sport in the US.   _____

10. Soccer has different rules in the US.   _____

New – Vocabulary: Emotions/Conditions

1.	Contento/Contenta	Happy
2.	Triste	Sad
3.	Emocionado/Emocionada	Excited
4.	Aburrido/Aburrida	Bored
5.	Deprimido/Deprimida	Depressed
6.	Feliz	Happy
7.	Cansado/Cansada	Tired
8.	Despierto/Despierta	Awake

30

40

50

60

70

80

90

100

Tired

Awake

Cuarenta   Treinta

Sesenta   Cincuenta

Ochenta   Setenta

Cien   Noventa

Despierto, Despierta   Cansado, Cansada

Depressed   Happy

Excited   Bored

Content   Toothbrush

Toothpaste   Deodorant

Comb   Socks

Feliz   Deprimido

Aburrido, Aburrida   Emocionado, Emocionada

El cepillo dental   Contento, Contenta

El desodorante   La crema dental

Los calcetines   El peine

Underwear   Belt

Pants   Hat

T-shirt   Painting

Towel   Breakfast

Lunch   Dinner

El cinturón   La ropa interior

La gorra   Los pantalones

El cuadro   La camiseta

El desayuno   La toalla

La cena   El almuerzo

Lesson 8

Lesson Highlights

Review
- A vs. An
- 3rd person

New
- Courtesy expressions
- 3rd person Q&A
- Free time
- Hotel Check-in

Review: A vs. An

Recuerda, la diferencia entre A y AN en inglés depende de las letras que empiezan el sustantivo que describe el artículo:

CONSONANTE	VOCAL
A banana	An apple

Esta  **regla solo aplica a la forma singular:**

What color is an apple?
An apple is red.

What color is a banana?
A banana is yellow.

En la forma plural, se usa la palabra SOME:

What color are some apples?
Some apples are red.

What color are some bananas?
Some bananas are yellow.

Let's practice!

Fill in the blank with the correct article. Then, answer the question!

What color is _____ orange?   _____

What color are _____ oranges?   _____

What color is _____ banana?   _____

What color are _____ bananas?   _____

What color is _____ onion?   _____

What color are _____ onions?   _____

What color is _____ avocado?   _____

What color are _____ avocados?   _____
What color is _____ blueberry?   _____
What color are _____ blueberries?   _____
What color is _____ eggplant?   _____
What color are _____ eggplants?   _____
What color is _____ coconut?   _____
What color are _____ coconuts?   _____

New: Equal rights for men and women.

Cuando se está describiendo a personas, los artículos y adjetivos no cambian por el género de la persona:

The secretary is happy. (Esta oración es igual para hombre y mujer). Vamos a leer el porqué en inglés abajo.

"We hold these truths to be self-evident, that all men are created equal, that they are endowed by their Creator with certain unalienable Rights, that among these are Life, Liberty and the pursuit of Happiness."   -The Declaration of Independence, July 4th, 1776

One of the best things about the United States is that it is a free country that supports equal rights for all of its citizens. This can be seen in the elimination of gender-based titles and a movement towards gender-neutral titles.

In the past, there were gender specific names for people in the United States. For example, a female server was called a waitress and a male server was called a waiter. Today, the job title is called a server and is the same for both men and women. In Latin America, employers typically specify "mesera" or "mesero" indicated the gender of the person they want to hire. This is illegal in the United States. Here are some other common examples:

Old term	New term
Fireman	Firefighter
Policeman	Police Officer
Mailman	Postal worker
Stewardess (Female)	Flight attendant
Steward (Male)	

New – Courtesy Expressions

- Muchas gracias – Thank you very much! Thanks a lot!
- De nada, mi amigo. – You're welcome, my friend.
- ¿Cómo? ¿Mande? – What/What did you say?
- Perdón. Disculpa. – I'm sorry. (En el sentido que cometiste un error)

- Lo siento. – I'm sorry. (De nuevo, si hiciste un error, pero también para expresar tu simpatía por una situación difícil por la cual una persona está pasando)
- Con permiso – Excuse me (cuando estás intentando pasar una persona o salir de la mesa o una reunión)

Let's practice! ¿Qué dirías en esta situación?

1. Alguien te acaba de ayudar a mudarte a tu casa nueva. _____
2. No oíste lo que alguien te acaba de decir. _____
3. Estás en una fiesta y quiere pasar entre varias personas. _____
4. Alguien te acaba de agradecer. _____
5. Te tropezaste contra alguien. _____
6. Un amigo te acaba de contar una noticia mala. _____
7. Acabas de ofender a alguien. _____
8. Tu patrón te acaba de aumentar el salario. _____

Review: 3rd person

Verbos S

Para decir que él/ella desea, agrega S
He/She wants

DESEAR – TO WANT/DESIRE		
Persona		Singular
1ª	I	Want
2ª	You	Want
3ª	He She	Wants

Verbos ES

Hay que agregar ES a los verbos que terminan con O o los que producen el sonido de S (S, SH, CH, X, ZZ)

Para decir que él/ella hace, agrega ES
He/She does

HACER – TO DO		
Persona		Singular
1ª	I	Do
2ª	You	Do
3ª	He She	Does

Verbos IES

Verbos que terminan con un consonante seguido por la letra Y tienen otra regla:
- Cambia la Y por I
- Agrega ES

Para decir que él/ella estudia, cambia la Y por I y agrega ES
He/She studies

ESTUDIAR – TO STUDY		
Person		Singular
1ª	I	Study
2ª	You	Study
3ª	He She	Studies

Complete the following verb charts with the correct form of the verb in English. Then complete the sentences that follow.

To talk		To walk	
I		I	
You		You	
He She		He She	

To do		To order	
I		I	
You		You	
He She		He She	

To study		To fly	
I		I	
You		You	
He She		He She	

To drink		To finish	
I		I	
You		You	
He She		He She	

To try		To press	
I		I	
You		You	
He She		He She	

To go		To fry	
I		I	
You		You	
He She		He She	

To teach		To fix	
I		I	
You		You	
He She		He She	

New – My daily routine

Para ésta actividad vamos a aprender unas nuevas palabras de vocabulario relacionadas con la rutina diaria.

1. **To arrive –Llegar**
2. **To have breakfast– Desayunar**
3. **To prepare, make –Preparar**
4. **To Rest – Descansar**
5. **Trabajar – To travel**
6. **Estudiar – To run**
7. **Responder – To respond, answer**
8. **Asistir – To attend**

Por is a preposition, and unfortunately prepositions are very tricky words to translate and can have multiple meanings.

Por = **Means of communication:**
- Hablo por teléfono – On the phone.
- Charlo por Facebook con mis amigo - By way of text message.
- Recibo cartas por correo - In the mail.

Por = **Expressing general movements and locations:**
- Ando por la calle - Around
- Pasas por el banco – By
- Mi vecino pasa por la puerta – Through

Por se usa también para expresar horas o periodos aproximados de tiempo, sin comienzo ni terminación específicos:

- **In (the morning, the afternoon)**
- **At (night, noon, midnight)**
- **Around, About**
- **During**
- ***"ISH"***

What do these sentences mean in Spanish?
1. Yo llego a casa por la tarde.

   _____
2. Tú asistes a las clases de inglés por la mañana.

   _____
3. Mi patrón responde a los empleados por la tarde.

   _____
4. Mi esposa desayuna por la mañana.

   _____
5. Yo trabajo por la noche.

   _____
6. Él prepara el café por la mañana.

   _____
7. Ella descansa por el mediodía.

   _____
8. Tú estudias inglés por el fin de semana.

   _____

Review - Time
What time is it?

10:10	9:17	8:24

_____   _____   _____

12:00	1:15	3:05

_____ _____ _____

4:25	5:35	7:56

_____ _____ _____

Review: Hotel check-in

Welcome to our hotel. How can I help you?
Hi, I need to _____ _____.

Of course, do you _____?
_____, My name is _____ _____.

How do you _____ your _____ _____?
It is spelled _____.

Perfect. Here it is. Your reservation is for 3 nights.
That is correct.

Do you have your ID and credit card?
Of course, _____ _____ _____.
Very well, _____ _____. Here is your _____. Enjoy your stay.
Thank you so much!

Thank you very much!   You're welcome, my friend!

What did you say?   I'm sorry for what I did.

I'm sorry for what I did.
I feel for you.   Excuse me.

To have breakfast   To arrive

                             To rest
To prepare   To not work

¡De nada, mi amigo!

¡Muchas gracias!

Perdón

Disculpa

¿Cómo?

¿Mande? (México)

Con permiso.

Lo siento.

Llegar

Desayunar

Descansar

Preparar

To work

To study

To respond

To answer

To attend

To go to

Do you have a reservation already?

Enjoy your stay!

The key

Very nice!

Preposition for approximate times:
- In (the morning, the afternoon)
- At (night, noon, midnight)
- Around, About
- During
- "Ish"

Welcome

Estudiar

Trabajar

Asistir

Responder

¡Disfruta su estancia!

¿Ya tiene reservación?

¡Muy amable!

La llave

Bienvenido
Bienvenida

Por

Lesson 9

Lesson Highlights

Review
- Hotel check-in
- Questions and answers
- 3rd person

New
- Tiempo libre (Free time)
- The American coffee shop
- 1st person plural (We)

New: Free time

Activities

1. Sing karaoke – Cantar karaoke
2. Listen to music – Escuchar música
3. Cook food – Cocinar comida
4. Garden – Trabajar en el jardín
5. Take pictures – Sacar fotos
6. Swim in the pool – Nadar en la piscina
7. Camp in the mountains – Acampar en las montañas
8. Sell things online – Vender cosas en línea
9. Hang out with friends – Pasar tiempo con amigos
10. Attend / Go to _____ games - Asistir a partidos de: Soccer, Baseball, Football, Basketball

To sing		To swim	
I		I	
You		You	
He She		He She	
To listen to		**To camp**	
I		I	
You		You	
He She		He She	
To cook		**To sell**	
I		I	
You		You	
He She		He She	
To garden		**To hangout**	
I		I	
You		You	
He She		He She	

To take (pictures)		To go to, attend	
I		I	
You		You	
He		He	
She		She	

Review: 3rd Person

1. David _____ (Attend) Rockies games.
2. My dad _____ (Camp) in the mountains.
3. My best friend _____ (Hang out) with me everyday.
4. My wife _____ (Cook) delicious food.
5. She _____ (Sell) clothes on Amazon.com.
6. My son _____ (Swim) in the pool.
7. Your mom _____ (Take) a lot of photos.
8. Maria _____ (Garden) on the weekend.
9. Your cousin _____ (Listen) to jazz music.
10. He _____ (Sing) karaoke every Friday.

New: 3rd Person - Questions

Imagínate que un amigo está preguntándote acerca de gente que conoces .
Ex:

• Does your best friend sing karaoke?
• Yes, he sings karaoke.

1. Sing karaoke
2. Listen to music
3. Cook food
4. Garden
5. Take pictures
6. Swim in the pool
7. Camp in the mountains
8. Sell things online
9. Hang out with friends
10. Attend / Go to Soccer/ Baseball/ Football/ Basketball games:

Your best friend
Your husband / wife
Your cousin
Your brother / sister
Your son / daughter
Your boss
Your teacher

Question: _____
Answer: _____

Question: _____
Answer: _____

Question: _____
Answer: _____

146

Question: _____
Answer: _____

Question: _____
Answer: _____

Question: _____
Answer: _____

Review: Questions - You and I

Imagínate que un amigo y tú se están haciendo preguntas:

Ex: Do you go to soccer games?   Yes, I go to soccer games.

Question: _____
Answer: _____

Question: _____
Answer: _____

Question: _____
Answer: _____

Question: _____
Answer: _____

Question: _____
Answer: _____

Question: _____
Answer: _____

Question: _____
Answer: _____

Question: _____
Answer: _____

Question: _____
Answer: _____

Question: _____
Answer: _____

Review - Hotel Check-in

Welcome to our hotel. How can I help you?

_____

Very well. Do you have a reservation?

_____

How do you spell your last name?

_____

Perfect. Here it is. Your reservation is for 3 nights.

_____

Do you have your ID and credit card?

_____

Very well, Mr(s) _____. Here is your key. Enjoy your stay.

Review: Numbers

1. How much does whisky cost?

   _____

2. How much does apple juice cost?

   _____

3. How much does a Coca-Cola cost?

   _____

4. How much does a bottle of sparkling water cost?

   _____

5. How much does gin cost?

   _____

6. How much does rum cost?

   _____

7. How much does orange juice cost?

   _____

8. How much does a bottle of still water cost?

   _____

Colorado Hotel MINIBAR Price List	
Whisky	$7.65
Gin	$6.75
Rum	$5.80
Juice	$3.50
Sparkling water	$2.30
Still water	$2.20
Soda	$2.95

New: Pronunciation

Si usted es del Caribe o de España, la J en inglés suena como la Y o la LL:

Jar - Yar   Joke - Yok
Jell-O - Yelo   Jury – Yuri
Jig - Yeg

La H produce el mismo sonido que la J en español:

Hay – Je   Hotel – Jotel
Help – Jelp   Hut – Hat
Hip – Jep

Por lo general, la Z en inglés se pronuncia diferente a la Z de español.

Si piensas en el sonido que hace un mosquito molesto que zumba y no te deja dormir, estarás muy cerca. En inglés, la z suena como un zumbido, como una s que haces vibrar con la lengua detrás de los dientes. Esta vibración se puede sentir también en la garganta. Suena más bien como la s de mismo, de rasguñar, o de paisano.

Como es un sonido menos común en español que en ingles, necesitas practicarlo bien. Repiten estas palabras en voz alta hasta que te sientas la vibración:

Zoo   Zany
Zig-zag   Zinc
Zipper   Zoom
Zebra   Zumba

New – 1st person plural - We

Ex: Want

Para cambiar los verbos dependiendo de quién está hablando, se cambia el sujeto más que el verbo.

Para decir nosotros deseamos, agrega WE: WE WANT

DESEAR – TO WANT	
Subject	
I You We	Want
He She	Wants

Para conversar, es más importante saber armar una pregunta, una respuesta positiva y una respuesta negativa. Es muy fácil en la primera persona plural:

- Pregunta: Do we speak English?
- Respuesta positiva: Yes, we speak English.
- Respuesta negativa: No, we do not speak English.

149

Let's practice!

1. He and I _____ (hablar) with his brother.
2. She and I _____ (caminar) every day.
3. David and I _____ (correr) very fast.
4. We _____ (ordenar) a hamburger.
5. We _____ (aprender) Spanish.
6. My sister and I _____ (vivir) in Denver.
7. Your cousin and I _____ (escribir) email.
8. We _____ (beber) a cold beer.
9. He and I _____ (comer) hot dogs.
10. She and I _____ (recibir) a lot of letters.

New: Questions and answers with We

Imagínate que estás hablando con tus compañeros de clase de inglés:

1. Do we talk English in class?

   _____

2. Do we want a vacation on the beach?

   _____

3. Do we do our homework?

   _____

4. Do we read the news?

   _____

5. Do we live in Denver?

   _____

6. Do we learn a lot in class?

   _____

7. Do we drink beer on the weekend?

   _____

8. Do we eat delicious food?

   _____

9. Do we attend Nuggets games?

   _____

10. Do we dance on the weekend?

   _____

New: 2nda persona singular con primera persona plural:

Hay otras maneras en las que la gente puede preguntarte algo que exige una respuesta con *we*. Vamos a aprender más preguntas y respuestas para *we*:

Si le preguntas a alguien qué hace con otra persona, recibirás una respuesta en la forma de *we*:

- ¿Qué haces con tu esposa?   What do you do with your wife?
- Nosotros hablamos de las noticias.   We talk about the news.

Let's practice!

1. What do you do with your husband/wife?
   _____

2. What do you do with your parents?
   _____

3. What do you do with your children?
   _____

4. What do you do with your brothers?
   _____

5. What do you do with your cousins?
   _____

6. What do you do with your colleagues?
   _____

7. What do you do with your boss?
   _____

8. What do you do with your friends?
   _____

9. What do you do with your pets?
   _____

10. What do you do with your neighbors?
   _____

New: The American coffee shop

A great place to go and practice your English is an American coffee shop, also called a *café*. Starbucks is one of the largest and most popular chains of cafés, but there are also many independent coffee shops. They typically sell not only a large variety of coffee, tea, and soft drinks, but also bread, pastries, sandwiches and snacks.

When you enter the café you go straight to the cashier, sometimes called a *barista*, to place your order. First, you order your drink from the large menu on the wall, and then choose your food from behind the glass display. The cashier will normally give you your food right away, but you may have to wait a few minutes while another barista makes your drink. You usually have to pick it up at the other end of the counter.

Americano
(Expreso y agua)

Cappuccino
(Café con espuma)

Latte
(Café con mucha leche)

Macchiato
(Café con caramelo)

Frappucino
(Café helado)

Iced tea
(Té helado)

Bagel - $1

Muffin - $.90

Croissant - $.80

Danish (pastry) -$1.30

Banana nut bread -$1.50

Breakfast sandwich - $3.50

Dialogue for the coffee shop

Customer – Hello, what is this called?
Barista - That is a muffin.

Customer – What flavor is it?
Barista – There is blueberry, banana or raisin.

Customer – How much is a muffin?
Barista – It is $.90.

Customer – What about these?
Barista – Those are Danishes, they cost $1.30.

Customer – Ok. I want a muffin and a Danish.
Barista – That will be $2.20. Anything else?

Customer – Yes, a large cappuccino, please.
Barista – Ok, that's fine. Your total is $7.00. For here or to go?

Customer – For here. Here is $10.
Barista – And here is your change, $3.00. Thank you! Have a nice day!

Let's practice!

Customer – _____

Barista – _____

Customer – _____

Barista – _____

Customer – _____

Barista – _____

Customer – _____

Barista – _____

Customer – _____

Barista – _____

Customer – _____

Barista – _____

Customer – _____

Barista – _____

Lesson 10

Lesson Highlights
Review
- I, You, He, She, We

New
- Pronunciation – la "K" muda
- 3rd person plural

Review: I, You,

1. Do you use a pen or pencil in class?

   _____

2. Do you swim in the pool often?

   _____

3. Do you live with roommates?

   _____

4. Do you prefer to communicate via text message or phone call?

   _____

5. Do you get a lot of friend requests on Facebook?

   _____

6. What music do you dance to?

   _____

7. Do you normally drink coffee or tea?

   _____

8. Do you travel a lot around Latinamerica?

   _____

9. Do you sell anything online?

   _____

10. Do you help poor people?

    _____

Review: 3rd person

1. Does the pastor say the Lord's Prayer?

   _____

2. Does your best friend talk too much?

   _____

3. Does your boss eat breakfast with you?

   _____

4. Does your spouse reserve flights for you?

   _____

5. Does the dog run with its owner?

   _____

6. Does the judge talk to the criminal?

7. Does your dad work too hard?

8. Does a baby drink milk?

9. Does your son learn a lot at school?

10. Does you rent go up every year?

Review: We

1. Do we read the dictionary a lot?

2. Do we study a lot of English?

3. Do we walk home after class?

4. Do we order Mexican food at the restaurant?

5. Do we drink a lot of Cuban rum?

6. Do we drive fast on the freeway?

7. Do we read books by Ernest Hemingway?

8. Do we make wine at home?

9. Do we arrive on time for class?

10. Do we get the day off on Federal holidays?

New: Pronunciation – La "K" muda

Hay muchas palabras con letras mudas en inglés, pero una de las más comunes es la "k" cuando viene a princpio de una palabra, y es seguida por la "n". En estos casos, la "k" no se pronuncia, es como si la palabra comenzara con la "n".

Repite en voz alta los ejemplos siguientes:

- Know
- Knee
- Kneel
- Knife
- Knit
- Knowledge

New – They – 3ra persona plural

La última conjugación verbal que vamos a aprender en este nivel es la 3ra persona plural para habla de lo que THEY (ELLOS/ELLAS) hacen.
Ex: Want

Para cambiar los verbos dependiendo de sobre quién estás hablando, se cambia el sujeto más que el verbo.

Para decir ellos/ellas desean, agrega
THEY: THEY WANT

De nuevo, para conversar, es más importante saber armar una pregunta, una respuesta positiva y una respuesta negativa. Es muy fácil en la tercera persona plural:

DESEAR – TO WANT	
Subject	
I You We They	Want
He She	Wants

- Pregunta: Do they want coffee?
- Respuesta positiva: Yes, they want coffee.
- Respuesta negativa: No, they do not want coffee.

Let's practice!

1. He and she _____ (hablar) with their brother.
2. She and he _____ (caminar) every day.
3. David y Luis _____ (correr) very fast.
4. They _____ (ordenar) a hamburger.
5. They _____ (aprender) Spanish.
6. My brothers _____ (vivir) in Denver.
7. Your cousins _____ (escribir) email.
8. They _____ (beber) a cold beer.
9. Steven and Rachel _____ (comer) hot dogs.
10. They _____ (recibir) a lot of letters.

Now, thinking about your parents….

1. Do they learn English?   _____
2. Do they order drinks?   _____
3. Do they run in the mountains?   _____
4. Do they walk in the park?   _____
5. Do they talk on the phone?   _____

And now the rest of the family….

1. Do your brothers live in Denver?

    _____

2. Do your cousins write a lot of message on Facebook?

3. Do your aunts and uncles drink beer?

_____

4. Do your children eat quesadillas?

_____

5. Do your neighbors get a lot of visitors?

_____

En inglés, la forma de **ustedes** es igual que la forma de **tú (You)**. Aunque la forma del verbo no cambie, en los Estados Unidos la gente dice un sujeto diferente dependiendo de la región. En el sur del país, se dice *Y'all* y en el noreste se dice *yous guys*. En otras partes del país es posible escuchar *you all* o *you guys*. Sin embargo, según las reglas de inglés, lo correcto es decir *you* tanto en la forma singular como en la plural.

Para establecer el contexto de la conversación, hay que nombrar las personas sobre quienes te estás refiriendo:

Q: What do your wife and you do?
Q: What do you do?
   A; We talk about the news.

- Si el contexto ha sido establecido, simplemente puedes decir *you*.
- La respuesta siempre será en la forma de *we*.

Let's practice!

Do you and your friends …

1. talk a lot? _____

2. walk in the mountains? _____

3. order pizza at home? _____

4. drink beer? _____

5. reserve hotels? _____

6. drink rum? _____

7. eat Indian food? _____

8. run together? _____

9. learn English? _____

10. live close? _____

11. write letters? _____

12. get presents? _____

English Foundations Final Exam

Name: _____   Date: _____

What does _____ mean?

1. Big _____
2. Little _____
3. Beautiful _____
4. Ugly _____
5. New _____
6. Old _____
7. Rich _____
8. Poor _____

How do you say _____?

9. Planta _____
10. Lápiz _____
11. Mesa _____
12. Marcador _____
13. Bolígrafo _____
14. Papel _____
15. Maestro _____
16. Estudiante _____

Contesta con oraciones completas:

1. How are you?

_____

2. What's your name?

_____

3. How do you spell your name?

_____

4. Where are you from?

_____

5. Where do you work?

_____

6. What is your phone number?

_____

7. How old are you?

_____

8. What do you like to do?

_____

Circle the most appropriate sentence:

1. I like tigers.   I like the tigers.
2. I like the dogs.   I like dogs.
3. I like the cats.   I like cats.
4. I like birds.   I like the birds.
5. I like fish.   I like the fish.
6. I like the horses.   I like horses.
7. I like hamburgers.   I like the hamburgers.
8. I like the beer.   I like beer.
9. I like cocktails.   I like the cocktails.
10. I like the soda.   I like soda.

What do you like?

1. _____
2. _____
3. _____

Agrega el artículo correcto: A/AN/SOME. Agrega un adjetivo adecuado.

1. ____ _____ Orange
2. ____ _____ Banks
3. ____ _____ Library
4. ____ _____ Letters
5. ____ _____ Park
6. ____ _____ Men
7. ____ _____ Women
8. ____ _____ Whiteboard
9. ____ _____ Dog
10. ____ _____ Apple
11. ____ _____ Cat
12. ____ _____ Watches
13. ____ _____ City
14. ____ _____ Aunts
15. ____ _____ Pencils
16. ____ _____ Windows
17. ____ _____ Door
18. ____ _____ Table
19. ____ _____ Chair
20. ____ _____ Telephone

Beautiful	Red
Ugly	Green
New	Yellow
Old	Blue
Big	Black
Small	Brown
Expensive	White
Cheap	Purple
Good	Pink
Bad	Grey

Ordering food

How can I help you?

_____

What do you want to drink?

_____

Do you want an appetizer?

_____

What do you want to eat?

_____

Do you want dessert?

_____

Is that all?

_____

Menu:

Drinks
Soda
Beer

Appetizers
Soup
Salad

Main course
Fried chicken
Hamburger

Dessert
Ice cream
Apple pie

Verbs:

Talk				
1st	I		We	
2nd	You			
3rd	He She		They	

Do				
1st	I		We	
2nd	You			
3rd	He She		They	

Study				
1st	I		We	
2nd	You			
3rd	He She		They	

1. I _____ (hablar) with his brother.
2. You _____ (caminar) everyday.
3. David and Luis _____ (correr) very fast.
4. We _____ (ordenar) a hamburger.
5. I _____ (aprender) Spanish.
6. My brothers _____ (vivir) in Denver.
7. You _____ (escribir) email.
8. He _____ (beber) a cold beer.
9. Rachel _____ (comer) hot dogs.
10. They _____ (recibir) a lot of letters.
11. Do you drink coffee in the morning?

_____

12. How many glasses of water do you drink normally?

_____

13. Do you eat fried chicken a lot?

_____

14. Where do you study English?

_____

15. Do you talk with your mom a lot?

_____

16. What do you do with your wife?

17. What do you do with your parents?

18. What do you do with your children?

19. What do you do with your siblings?

20. What do you do with your cousins?

21. Does your grandpa live in Denver?

22. Does your grandma write poetry?

23. Does your mom get email?

24. Does your dad get junk mail?

25. Does your brother live in a house?

Reading – New York

New York is located in the northeastern part of the United States and is the largest city by population with more than 8 million residents. It has the largest Jewish population in the Americas. New York is a true "melting pot" of cultures and about half of the people speak a language other than English. It is well known for its Italian American residents and many believe New York style pizza to be the best in the world. The architecture is amazing and consists of some of the tallest skyscrapers in the world, like the Empire State Building. New York has all types of sports teams, including soccer, 2 hockey teams, 2 basketball teams, and 2 baseball teams. Many consider it to be the greatest city in the world.

True or false?
1. New York City is a small city.   _____
2. More than 8 million people live in New York.   _____
3. The Jewish religion is not important in New York.   _____
4. Sports are very popular in New York.   _____
5. New York doesn't have good pizza.   _____
6. There is nothing interesting to see in New York.   _____

Made in the USA
Monee, IL
21 July 2021